HISTORICAL HOSTELRIES

A GUIDE TO THE HISTORIC PUBS
OF SHREWSBURY
BETWEEN THE BRIDGES

Nigel Hinton & David Trumper

Historical Hostelries

The guide to provide you with up to date information on the historic pubs of Shrewsbury between the bridges, together with a summary of some history of the buildings, landlords, customers and other aspects of the various pubs still trading in the spring of 2005.

First published in 2005

This edition is published by Nigel Hinton 4 Darwin Court Oxon Business Park Shrewsbury SY3 5AL

ISBN 0-9550343-0-2

Front Cover......The Kings Head Mardol, one of the oldest pubs in town, next to the Bedroom, under the shade one of the newest.

Back Cover........The Loggerheads

Printed in Great Britain by Creative Digital Printing, Shrewsbury, SY3 5DD

CONTENTS

MAP OF SHREWSBURY

Start at the station and follow   . . . .

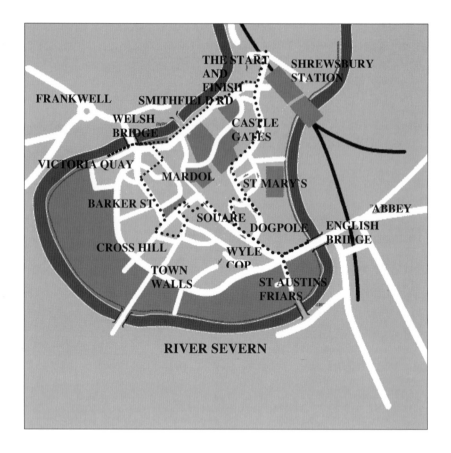

ABOUT THE AUTHORS

Nigel Hinton

Nigel Hinton is a Chartered Accountant. He has lived and worked in Shrewsbury for almost 30 years with his wife Bridget. They have three daughters Catharine, Bethany and Susanna and grandchildren Merlin, and Poppy who all live and work in Shrewsbury. Nigel has a wide range of interests including golf, music, motor sport, salsa dance and archaeology. The latter interests are shared with Bridget and together they made a small contribution to the award winning Wroxeter Hinterland Project with Dr Roger White and have assisted with guided tours around Wroxeter. Bridget is a green badge Shrewsbury Town Guide.

David Trumper

David Trumper is Shrewsbury born and bred. After leaving school he worked for several years in the printing industry before training as a teacher. After 30 years teaching in various schools around the county he took early retirement. David has written 11 books about the local history of Shropshire. He contributes articles to local magazines, gives slide shows and lectures about the county's past to a wide variety of organisations, and he also arranges historic walks in the area. David is married to Wendy and they have a daughter Vicki married to Andrew and a grandson Sam.

This book is Nigel and David's first joint venture. It is hoped it will be followed by others featuring the historic buildings and characters of Shrewsbury and Shropshire.

AUTHORS' ACKNOWLEDGMENTS

The authors are grateful for the assistance received from the staff of Records and Research for their help in accessing material for the book and also to the staff of the Shrewsbury Museums' Service for information on William Rowley..

Thanks to David Benson and David Woodhouse for the loan of historic post cards and we acknowledge the use made of "The Inns of Shrewsbury" by L.C.Lloyd.

This book would not have been published without the help of all of the landlords and managers of the pubs between the bridges named in the current information. We are also grateful to Irving Stewart and Mark Brawn for the assistance in production and the printers Messrs Creative Digital Printing of Oxon, Shrewsbury and to Ros Ephraim of Burway Books and Dorothy Nicole for their assistance with developing the idea.

We are also extremely grateful for the support given to us by our respective families over the years we have been involved in the research on this project.

The future of the licensed trade

The licensed trade has been subject to constant change since regulations began in times past and there is no doubt it will continue to evolve in the future.

At the time of writing the Licensing Act 2003 is progressively coming in to force and a number of pubs have obtained licences for non standard hours, this means that they can stay open until the early hours of the morning 2 or 3 am. Also all premises licences authorising the supply of alcohol must have an identified individual licence holder who will act as supervisor of licensed premises.

In the last fifty years there has been amalgamation and consolidation of smaller regional breweries into international brands that can be obtained almost anywhere in the world and marketing is a major cost in the price of a pint. The traditional cask conditioned pint has been under considerable threat, however in Shropshire we are fortunate that we have a number of local breweries these include Hanby Ales, Wem. Hobson's Brewery, Cleobury Mortimer. Six Bells, Bishops Castle. The Wood Brewery, Wistanstow. The Sun Inn, Corvedale. John Roberts Brewery, Bishops Castle. Salopian Brewery, Shrewsbury. Do your best to support them.

Shrewsbury and West Shropshire CAMRA

Organisers of the Shrewsbury Real Ale Festival

Early September

The Music Hall, the Square, Shrewsbury.

The branch has over 400 members and has operated in the area for over thirty years. For more information contact www.shrewsburycamra.org.uk
Branch Contact is Nigel Bevan Secretary   nigel@bevan.com

PREFACE

Shrewsbury has long been the centre of defence, pilgrimage, trade, and administration as the county town of Shropshire. Today the army and pilgrims are less important but the town continues to be an administration centre, important historic tourist attraction, and a busy market town with a mix of shopping centres and individual specialist retailers.

There is evidence of religious pilgrimage and markets being held in the heart of the town from Norman times, next to St Alkmunds the Kings market thrived. Later in the 14th and 15th centuries when Shrewsbury had a virtual monopoly of the wool trade and the Drapers built the Market Hall with a charter from Elizabeth 1. Other charters were granted and these markets attracted traders, farmers, shoppers, drovers and pack horse trains who brought farm produce, woollen cloth and skins to be traded at market. To accommodate these visitors the town was liberally sprinkled with lodging houses, pubs, and inns offering basic accommodation and refreshment. Over the course of the last five centuries around 120 hostelries have been recorded between the bridges.

The centre of Shrewsbury is little more than half a mile square and is virtually surrounded by the River Severn which once provided its protection, and the major import and export route down stream to Bristol and beyond. A major inland port operated at the bottom of Mardol and in Frankwell. In those days "bow hauliers" manually pulled the boats known as "Trows" up stream. These brought wine and spirits and other luxury goods to the town, woollen cloth and other products where exported. There were two major bridges into the town where tolls were collected, the English Bridge and the Welsh Bridge. Anything within the river loop is said to be "between the bridges".

Today there are nearly ninety licensed premises trading "between the bridges" but many of these are hotels and restaurants, which we have not included in this guide. We hope to feature Historical Hotels and Historical Restaurants in future publications!

As we see from the brief look at the history of the remaining pubs in town today there is constant change often dictated by trends and changes in fashion; and more recently increased legislation and a new awareness of the health implications of drinking alcohol. The independent Landlord is under threat, an endangered species, and needs your support. Since the idea for this book was originally mooted in 2003 the town centre has lost the Elephant and Castle in Mardol and the Plough in the Square. Many more pubs in the suburbs and villages have followed a national trend and become housing developments.

Shrewsbury is very fortunate as it still boasts a number of traditional pubs and inns well worth visiting. It has been a daunting task to explore the hostelries of Shrewsbury, and to sample their fare, in the interests of accuracy, but someone had to do it!

We trust you will enjoy using this guide and hope it prompts you to visit some of the most historic buildings in Shrewsbury. Whatever your tastes, in either ale or food you can find it here and if at first you do not succeed, try, try and try again.

INTRODUCTION TO THE WALK

We have only covered the pubs within the loop of the river "between the bridges" currently trading in May 2005. We hope at some time to turn our attentions to those other excellent establishments outside the bridges

The idea of a pub walk is not original but it's a good one! Join us as we take a walk around the town centre pubs and perhaps you will try one that you have not been in before. One or two landmarks will be mentioned but this is not intended to be a full guided tour of the town. You can pick up the route at any point you like, but we are starting, and finishing, at the Railway Station

THE STATION & CASTLE GATES

Opposite the Railway Station is the Albion and the Station Hotel. Then walk up Castle Gates and find on your left the Bulls Head and then the Vaults. Continuing up Castle Gates, and turning left at the Post Office, by the High Cross, brings you into St Mary's Street. Immediately opposite the Post Office you will find the Yorkshire House.

ST MARY'S & BUTCHER ROW

Return to St Mary's Street, turn left, and a walk a hundred yards to find Cromwell's on your right. Retrace your steps to Church Street, and there you will find the Loggerheads on your left. Opposite is Chambers that is part of the Prince Rupert Hotel. Walk to the bottom of Church Street and turn right towards Butcher Row to find the main entrance to the Prince Rupert Hotel and next door is the Bull. Almost opposite is Owens Wine Bar. Walk back a few yards, and turn right into Fish Street and at the far end on the right is the Three Fishes.

WYLE COP & ENGLISH BRIDGE

Continue down Fish Street to the High Street, and turn left down the hill called Wyle Cop - where on the left hand side you will find the Nags Head. From here you can easily spot the Lion Hotel opposite. At this stage cross the road, carefully! Continue down Wyle Cop, and at the bottom of the hill you can see Tanners award winning wine merchants opposite. Continue on towards the English Bridge to the Lion and Pheasant. Turn back and turn first left, opposite Tanners Wines, into St Julian's Friars, where you will find the Hop and Friar. Turn round, and go back up the Cop and at Barracks Passage just before the Lion Hotel turn left and you find the Old Lion Tap.

HIGH STREET

Come back out of the passage and carry straight on up the Cop into the High Street and you will come to the Wheatsheaf on your left on the corner of High Street and Milk Street; in Milk Street itself is the Old Post Office. Head back into High Street, turn left, and follow it down a few yards. On your left is Golden Cross Passage. You will not be surprised to find the Golden Cross Hotel at the end of it! Returning to the High Street you will find Baileys Venue Bar to the left. Continue on to the Square.

AROUND THE SQUARE AND BEYOND SHOPLATCH

Sadly there are no pubs left in the Square, but a few survive close by.

To the right of the Old Market Hall built in1596, and near a Victorian pillar box are some steps leading into Gullet Passage. On the left at the bottom of the passage is the Hole in the Wall with its entrance on Shoplatch. Turn left, walk a few yards, and then left again into Market Street. From there turn right into Swan Hill to find the Admiral Benbow. Further up Swan Hill on the corner of Cross Hill is the Coach and Horses. Go down Cross Hill, right into St. John's Hill, and return to Shoplatch.

BELLSTONE & BARKER STREET

On the corner of Shoplatch and Bellstone we find the Exchange. Now head towards the big timber frame building, Rowley's museum. On the left is the Bellstone, a few yards further on you'll find Rowley's on the same side, it is opposite the timber framed building it gets its name from. Cross the street, and beyond the car park you will see Lloyds. To the left of Lloyds there is a narrow passage Caernarvon Lane which leads into the old part of town known as Mardol.

MARDOL AND SMITHFIELD ROAD

Cross the narrow street, turn right, to discover the Kings Head and immediately next door is The Bedroom, about twenty yards further up is Yates's wine bar. Do a "U-turn" and head back down Mardol towards the river. At the junction with the Smithfield Road you will find the Shrewsbury Hotel, facing the river and the bridge. Walk past the Shrewsbury Hotel car park, cross the wide street by the lights, and follow the route of the river for about a hundred yards, to discover the Armoury on your left.

Retrace your steps to the bottom of Mardol and then continue on Smithfield Road keeping the river to your left continue for about fifty yards and you will find the Soho bar. Continue along Smithfield Road and you will arrive at the Albert and the end of the journey!

Using the guide, you can pause and take a rest when and where you need it. This walk can be done within an hour or can be done in stages over many years. You select the pace and the places to take refreshment.

THE ALBION c.1856

A convenient place to meet rail and bus travellers and visitors. This pub has a well established landlord who has a loyal following of regulars.

Theme	A traditional Town Pub
Opening Hours	Mon - Sat 11.00 - 11.00 Sunday 12.00 - 10.30
Licensee	Terry Lewis
Address	Castle Foregate, Shrewsbury, Shropshire SY1 2DJ
Contact	01743 354906
Brewery	Burtonwood
House Beers	Burtonwood / Banks's, Carling, Stella, Guinness, Strongbow on draft.
Real Ales	No
Food	Sunday Lunch Special see A Boards
Wines	Brewery selection
Promotions	Various Special Brewery Offers
Entertainment	TV, Darts & Dominoes
Accommodation	3 twin rooms and 1 single
Awards	Pub of the Year 1996. Has won many Town of Flowers awards for its attractive window displays.
Customers	Mainly over 25 years old with the regulars travelling from outside the centre of Shrewsbury. Postmen, railwaymen, commuters, and travellers continue to be the main customers.
Comment	You will receive a warm welcome from Terry who has established a successful trade with a quality product.

THE ALBION HOTEL HISTORY

The Albion was officially recorded for the first time in 1856. There is some speculation whether the licence was transferred there from the Fighting Cocks, which stood on the opposite side of the road and which was demolished to facilitate the building of the railway station. This is confirmed by an advert in the Salopian Journal dated 25th August 1847 announcing the sale of the furniture, *"in consequence of the premises being wanted for the Railway Station."*

Photo: The Albion Castle Foregate 1960

The Fighting Cocks certainly lived up to its name as one local in the 1840s remembers seeing a man carrying several dead and mutilated birds out of the inn and throwing them into a cart.

The name Albion is the popular and patriotic name for England and there are many inns of this name spread throughout the country. In 1900 the owner and landlord was Thomas Chester who bought the inn on 4th October 1883. At the turn of the century the Albion had eight private rooms, three public rooms, and accommodation for eight people in four double rooms. The customers at this time were described as *"working class people and railway officials"*.

Nigel's Notes: "Good Ale! You are my darling; you are my joy both night and morning" Traditional Song

THE STATION HOTEL c.1828

This pub is convenient to visitors to the town centre, which has recently changed hands and has been refurbished. It is now benefiting from an enthusiastic new landlady.

Theme	Refurbished Traditional Town Pub
Opening Hours	Mon - Sat 10.30 - 11.00 Sun 12.00 - 10.30
Licensee	Glynis Lanning
Address	Castle Foregate, Shrewsbury, Shropshire, SY7 9DJ
Contact	T. 01743 344505
Brewery	Punch Taverns
House Beers	Tetley, Worthington, Carling, & Extra Cold, Guinness, Stella, & Strongbow.
Real Ales	None
Food	Food is always available. A flexible menu operates with seasonal produce and meals can be booked as required.
Wine	House wine
Promotions	Doubles £3
Entertainment	TV, Dartboard & Dominoes
Accommodation	None
Awards	None
Customers	A wide age range of regulars.
Comments	This pub is a convenient meeting place close to the bus and railway stations.

THE STATION HOTEL'S HISTORY

This inn was first recorded as the Grapes in 1828 and once sported a very fine cast-iron bunch of grapes over the Castle Foregate entrance. It retained that name until 1939. When the old Station Hotel on the corner of Castle Gates and Meadow Place was demolished, to make way for the Granada Cinema, the name was transferred. The original inn was housed in a much older timber-framed building which was burnt down in January 1856, soon after the landlord Henry Birchall had taken over. The alarm was raised by the bells of St. Mary's Church being rung in "reverse peals". The fire was fought by two engines from the Salop Fire Office, one from the North Wales Office, and the Station and Factory engines. Hundreds of townspeople were also on hand to render assistance. Although the fire fighters were criticised by some sections of the public because they were slow to respond and their apparatus was inadequate, it was generally agreed that the inn could not be saved. The "helpers" did manage to save a great deal of Mr. Birchall's property; but the next day the Chief Constable was forced to issue a handbill requesting people to return the items they had "rescued". During the chaos a thief masquerading as a helper, managed to make off with a box belonging to Mrs Birchall, which contained £4-15s. The "helpers" also managed to consume over twelve gallons of spirits while tackling the blaze!

During the last twenty years of the nineteenth century the owner and landlord was Richard Ince who was also the proprietor of the Salopian Tin & Zinc Works; which he managed from the rear of his premises in Chester Street. In the Kelly's Directory of 1891 he advertised both businesses in this way.

The Salopian Tin & Zinc Works. *"Wholesale & Retail Tin, Iron, Zinc, Brass, Wire & Copper-plate Worker. All kinds of petroleum & moderator lamps cleaned and repaired. Beer engines fixed & repaired. Gas fittings & repairs executed. Estimates given for all types of gas and water work. Tea urns for hire. All jobs neatly executed on the shortest notice. The Grapes Hotel & Posting House. Opposite the General Railway Station. Commercial visitors will find every accommodation on most reasonable terms. Ales, wines & spirits of superior quality, Choice cigars. Good stabling & cart room. Proprietor Richard Ince."*

By 1900 the hotel comprised five private and eight public rooms, with accommodation in two rooms for eight people. But by this date all stabling of horses had gone. There were five entrances into the building, one in Chester Street, one in Castle Foregate, and three into a passage that led to Chester Street.

During the Second World War the landlord was Walter Smith who did his best to boost moral by decorating his bar with old matchboxes.

Photo: The Grapes c.1921

15

THE BULLS HEAD c.1832

A town centre pub conveniently situated to both train and bus stations.

Theme   Traditional Town Pub

Opening Hours   Mon - Sat 11.00 - 11.00 Sun 12.00 - 10.30

Licensee   Glen Leversedge

Address   Castle Gates, Shrewsbury, Shropshire, SY1 2AB

Contact   T. 01743 344148

Brewery   Banks's

House Beers   Banks's Bitter and Mild, Carlsberg, Guinness, Fosters, Stella, Strongbow and Woodpecker.

Real Ales   None

Food   Crisps and snacks available

Wine   Stowells wines

Promotions   Double Specials – Bells, Bacardi and Smirnov £2.10

Entertainment   Pool, Darts

Accommodation None

Awards   None

Customers   Wide age range of regulars including postmen, rail workers, and visitors. Pool and Darts players are also catered for.

Comments   A traditional town centre pub offering value and service.

THE BULLS HEAD HISTORY

Although Castle Gates only stretches from the steps of the Dana down to the entrance to the railway station, it has in its history had ten public houses recorded along its short frontage. The Bulls Head was first listed in 1832, and has kept its original name throughout its history! The building itself dates from the early years of the 19th century and it was built close to the site of the northern gateway into Shrewsbury which passed through the old town defences. The foundations of the building were erected over the defensive ditch, which has caused subsidence, leaving some of the windows in the upper storeys at very odd angles. Around the time this inn opened, another with the same name in Castle Street closed. The old inn had a very fine carved sign over the entrance, which was transferred to the new premises, to stand over the front door until about 1874.

From around 1850 until the late 1870s carrier wagons from Hawkestone, High Ercall, and other areas in the north of the county used the Bull's Head as their headquarters and as a terminus for passengers. The carriers were the early form of the county bus service

16

providing transport to the county town from outlying villages on certain days of the week, and also carrying vital goods and necessary items. In 1856 four carriers used the inn, including two women;

Photo: The Bulls Head Castle Gates 1903.

Ann Phillips worked between Shrewsbury and Grinshill on a Saturday, and Sarah Wood between the county town and Hardwicke on Wednesdays. In 1886 the proprietor of the inn was R.F. Morris who advertised *"Celebrated Manchester Ales, wines and spirits of the finest quality, well aired beds, and refreshments of every description on the shortest notice."*

By 1900 the inn was owned by Yates & Co. of the Castle Brewery Birkenhead. The customers at this time were described as railway workers, cabmen and the working class. During their visits they were able to amuse themselves with a game of bagatelle.

THE VAULTS c.1829

The new owners are aiming for quality, value and customer satisfaction!

Theme	Traditional Town Pub
Opening Hours	Mon - Sat 12- 11 Sunday 12.10.30
Licensee	Mary Lambert & Adrian Long
Address	16 Castle Gates, Shrewsbury, SY1 2AB
Contact	T. 01743 358807
	www.thevaults.co.uk
Brewery	Free house,
House Beers	London Pride, Deuchars IPA guest beers change regularly with customer demand but will usually include one local brewery.
Real Ales	Yes
Food	Bar food and restaurant areas under refurbishment.
Wine	House wines and a good world choice
Promotions	
Entertainment	Sociable level of live music all weekend. Multi-level outside seating under the historic castle walls.
Accommodation	8 letting rooms, singles, doubles & twin rooms all en suite available soon.
Awards	None yet
Customers	Attracts all over 21 age groups looking for a good night out. Some dress restrictions..

THE VAULT'S HISTORY

The inn was first recorded in 1829 and was known as either the Castle Inn or Castle Vaults until around 1999, when it became Brady's Bar. In January 2005 it was renamed the "Vaults". The building was erected at the start of the nineteenth century and features an attractive front with arched windows and pilasters. It originally occupied number sixteen but was later extended to include number seventeen. In February 1836 William Blakeway, the landlord of the Turf Inn on Claremont Hill, took over the Castle Inn from Mr. S. Surman. In an advert he *"Begs respectfully to inform his friends, agricultural gentlemen, and the public in general that he has entered upon the above old and established inn and assures them that no excursion will be wanting as it is his determination to unite comfort with moderate charges and hopes by civility and attention to obtain a share of their support. Well aired beds, excellent stabling and good hay and corn"*. Three years later the inn was again on the market and advertised as *"advantageously situated opposite the great Chester Road and now in full and profitable business. On the ground floor the building consists of a large and small dining parlour, a large and convenient bar, an excellent kitchen, market room, scullery, and convenient brew house. On the first floor a large sitting room and four good bedrooms; and in the attic another four bedrooms capable of holding more than twenty beds.*

Under the large parlour were a good-sized cellar and a large vault. To the rear of the house a lower yard and an extensive upper yard with two stables containing fourteen stalls.

Photo: The Castle Vaults c.1960

There are also three undivided stables, a shed with haylofts, gig house and a small garden. The public are also informed that the house and shop next door are also up for sale and that with the 'probability' that the intended railroad terminus will be immediately adjoining, will render the already thriving and populous neighbourhood the most desirable about Shrewsbury for profitable investment."

Towards the end of the 19th century Mrs L. Halfpenny owned the inn before it was taken over by her son William. In 1886 Mrs Halfpenny advertised the Castle Hotel as having: *"Good accommodation for visitors and commercial gentlemen. Close to the railway station and within a minute's walk of the Smithfield".*

She also kept a good supply of Bass Ales and Combes Stout and operated a store selling local families the finest quality wines and spirits at moderate prices. Henry Burnett who lived on the Ellesmere Road owned the Castle in 1900 and it remained privately owned until 1948 when the Wrekin Brewery of Wellington bought it.

In recent years it has been known for selling Mexican food, and for being an Irish Bar.

THE YORKSHIRE HOUSE c.1828

A centrally located beer and cider house set in a delightful timbered building offering a lively night out with some of the best beer and cider available in Shrewsbury.

Theme	Traditional beer and cider house.
Opening Hours	Mon- Sat 11.00 – 11.00 Sun 12.00 – 10.30
Licensee	Paul Bailey
Address	St. Mary's Place, Shrewsbury, Shropshire, SY1 1DX
Contact	T. 01743 362622
Brewery	Punch Taverns
House Beers	Kronenburg 1664, Worthington Creamflow, Draft Guinness, Stella Artois, Ciders include Strongbow, Scrumpy Jack, Woodpecker.
Real Ales	Old Speckled Hen, IPA Greene King,
Food	Simple snacks available
Wine	Fair selection
Promotions	Good quality at all times.
Entertainment	Juke box and regular live bands
Accommodation	None
Awards	None
Customers	Draft cider and beer drinkers, rockers and bikers, and everyone that enjoys Rock Music
Comments	A lively night out if you are in the mood to rock.

THE YORKSHIRE HOUSE HISTORY

 The Yorkshire House was first recorded as a public house in 1828, although its history dates further back than this, as it was the home of a social club in the early part of the eighteenth century. When far from home people from an area liked to meet and it is thought that in the past, exiles from Yorkshire used to seek each other's company at this house, perhaps even at the social club.

The inn is situated in an old timber-framed building that was later encased in brick sometime in the 18th century. Parts of the cellar are much older and have dressed stonewalls from the 13th century, similar to stone work in St. Mary's, and may be part of the outbuildings of the church.

In 1851 it was the terminus for the Withington Carrier, Thomas Leary, who travelled between the town and village on Wednesdays and Saturdays.

For many years the inn remained in private ownership, and was one of the last public houses in Shrewsbury to sell its own home-brewed ale, until the 1930s.

Photo: The Yorkshire House St Mary's Place c.1960

In 1900 the owner and landlord was John Lowe and the public house consisted of ten rooms; six private and four public, with overnight accommodation for ten people in three rooms

The most famous landlord of the Yorkshire House was Gerald Cuff, who arrived in July 1959 with his dog Janey. He was fifty-four at the time and had been an actor for over twenty-seven years before becoming a landlord in Wolverhampton. His best known role was as the 'Bos'un' in ITV' s popular 'Popeye Show,' which had started eighteen months before he came to Shrewsbury.' Every Monday he would leave Shrewsbury to travel to the television studios in Birmingham to present another live show.

CROMWELLS c.1950

A lively quality restaurant, wine bar, and hotel.

Theme	Relaxed bar and restaurant
Opening Hours	Mon-Sat 11am-11pm Sun 12noon -10.30pm
Licensee	Not given
Address	11 Dogpole, Shrewsbury, Shropshire, SY1 1EN
Contact	T.01743 361440 F. 01743 341121
	www.cromwellsinn.com / www.inncompanygroup.co.uk
Brewery	Inn Company Group
House Beers	Always at least 2 local guest ales available.
Real Ales	Yes
Food	Some of the best cuisine with inspirational dishes prepared from traditionally produced local ingredients at the height of their flavour. The food offers an eclectic blend of a la carte, bar food and splendid family Sunday lunches
Wine	Good selection of various wines
Promotions	Contact hotel for current offers.
Entertainment	Live music – outside seating
Accommodation	Four double bedrooms 2 twin and the option of a family room that have all been recently refurbished with consideration to many original features.
Awards	None
Customers	An eclectic mix of drinkers and diners looking for quality.
Comments	Cromwell's has built a solid local reputation for quality. The barbeque on the Terrace is best enjoyed in fine weather. The coffee in the restaurant is Illy Espresso especially imported from Italy.

CROMWELLS HISTORY

Until the middle of the 20th century the building was a private house. In 1886 it was occupied by L.J.R. Oxley a dental surgeon and from around 1917 until the Second World War by the Misses Lloyd. It was then transformed into the Warwick, a private residential hotel initially run by H. Bradbury. The hotel then passed to F. and E. Trow who advertised

"A licensed restaurant with a full menu and fresh salads" The accommodation offered was described as fairly basic, just bed and breakfast, with hot and cold running water and an electric fire in each room.

Beneath the plaster on the outside of the hotel is a fine early 17th century timber-framed building, which blends in well with other buildings on the street. The interior also contains many of its original features including a great deal of panelling, and a fine Jacobean staircase.

Photo: Cromwells when it was a private house c. 1920

In 1961 the hotel was sold for £6000 to a London development company who wanted to demolish the old building and erect a new office and showroom on the site. There was a huge protest and a preservation order was placed on the building by the Borough Council. A counter petition was put up by the developers, which led to a Ministry of Housing and Local Government Inquiry, held at the Castle on 7th November 1961. The argument by both the architect and the consultant engineer for the developers was that the building was unsafe. They thought that it would cost around £10,000 to put the building back into a fit state of repair and if a heavy wind blew they would be very worried about the consequences. They argued that the front of the building was *'an abortion'*, and described the area of Dogpole where, the house stands, as *'not attractive and on either side of the building there are places of no outstanding character. 'It is a bastard street."*

Mr. A.T. Morris the Borough Surveyor said, *'To demolish Shrewsbury's old Warwick Hotel would be little short of vandalism'*. He also told the Inquiry that it wasn't uncommon in timber-framed buildings for the chimney breasts and walls to be out of plumb, for doors and windows to be out of alignment, and floors slightly tilted. He argued that having stood for several hundred years, with ordinary maintenance, it should stand for many more. Mr. Ronald Milton an architect, who owned the property next to the hotel, pointed out to the Inquiry that the difference between renovation or demolition was only £50; and the house having such a prominent position on Dogpole would mean that *'much of the character of the street would be lost if it was demolished.'*

After three months of deliberation the Inspector came down on the side of the Borough Council. Although he agreed with the developers that they would get a better return if the site were redeveloped he said they had been under no obligation to buy it. He then recommended the preservation order be confirmed because of the building's appearance, its unspoilt character, its special architectural and historic interest, and the adverse affect demolition would have on the character and appearance of Dogpole.

Within two months the property was sold for an undisclosed amount to Jack Williams and was transformed into a health food shop and cafe called Healthiways.

THE SHREWSBURY ARMS c.1780
(AKA THE LOGGERHEADS)

A traditional beer house offering consistently high quality products over several decades. The CAMRA awards span many years and speak volumes to the discerning traditional beer drinker.

Theme	Traditional 18th century beer house
Opening Hours	Mon - Sat 11.00-11.00 Sun 12.00 - 3.00 8.00 - 10.30
Licensee	Robin Walker
Address	Church Street, Shrewsbury, Shropshire, SY1 1UG
Contact	T. 01743 355457. F. 01743 270534
Brewery	Banks's
House Beers	Banks's Original, Marstons Pedigree, Bass. Guest Beers changed regularly. Guinness & Strongbow
Real Ales	Guests
Food	Bar snacks available.
Wine	Brewery options.
Promotions	None
Entertainment	Impromptu live music on a Thursday.
Accommodation	None
Awards	CAMRA 2004 Pub of the Year and also winner of a Little altered interiors award.
Customers	Anyone who enjoys a traditional pint in an historic location with scrubbed pine tables and tile floors will enjoy a visit to the Loggerheads.
Comments	Virtually unaltered historic interior. If you like beer in an original setting you will like this pub. Look out for Poets' corner.

THE SHREWSBURY ARMS HISTORY

The inn is in the rear section of an old building on the corner of St. Mary's Street and Church Street. It has a brick shell over an earlier stone structure and is thought to date from the latter half of the 17th century. Although its early history is unknown it has been recorded as a public house since 1780 when it was known as the Greyhound. Later it was renamed the Horse and Jockey, and then the Lord Hill or the General Lord Hill after Shropshire's most famous soldier. In 1828 the inn was renamed the Shrewsbury Arms but has been known locally by its "nickname", the Loggerheads, since 1831.

The Loggerheads is the name given to the three leopard, or lion heads, depicted on the arms of the town. Several explanations have been put forward as to how the name arose. The most likely is that it's a corruption of 'Lubbar's Head' the old English for a leopard's head. In his play Henry II Part Two, Shakespeare refers to Falstaff being invited to a dinner at the 'Lubbar's Head', in Lombard Street.

Photo: The Shrewsbury Arms "Loggerheads" Church St 1960

Another explanation put forward by R.F. Prideaux (a former town clerk) is that the word is much older, derived from the Norman 'l'orge', unpleasant spectre

Local knowledge is always important when referring to place names. In 2004 the brewery put up an inn sign depicting a turtle wrongly believing that a loggerhead referred to one of those species.

The inn was sold by auction on the 9th May 1822 and advertised as *'All that old established and much frequented public house and premises known by the sign of General Lord Hill, now in the occupation of Mr. Thomas Williams. The situation is central and the premises are in excellent repair. To any person desirous of making a good thing of the business by keeping a superior tap of home brewed ale, or to a maltster or brewer desirous of securing the custom of a good house, a most advantageous opportunity presents itself'.* In August 1831 the inn was advertised to let after the landlord, Mr. Brindley auctioned off all his household furniture, brewing vessels and around 140 gallons of ale.

By 1900 the inn was owned by T. Cooper & Co. of Burton-on-Trent. The landlord was Joseph Russell and the house consisted of three public and nine private rooms. There was also accommodation for ten people in three bedrooms.

THE PRINCE RUPERT HOTEL c.1950

A centrally located comfortable hotel surrounded by cobbled streets. Ideal base from which to explore the town's historic attractions only a few steps away. Chambers Brasserie attached to the hotel offers good value bistro food.

Theme	A traditional English market town centre hotel
Opening Hours	Hotel is open all hours
Licensee	Michael Matthews
Address	Butcher Row Shrewsbury
Contact	01743 499955
	www.prince-rupert-hotel.co.uk
Brewery	Free House
House Beers	Limited range of keg and bottled beer.
Real Ales	No
Food	The restaurant offers an excellent Table d`haute and A la Carte Menus
Wines	Tanners wines offering world wide options with some fine vintages available.
Promotions	Weekend Breaks
Entertainment	None
Accommodation	70 Tastefully furnished en suite rooms including 12th century oak beamed suites, four-poster canopied beds and deluxe rooms. All have TV, hairdryer and tea/coffee making tray.
Other Facilities	Conferences and formal dinners
Awards	Silver Swan Award for excellence.
	2 RAC Dining Awards
Customers	A wide range of guests including stars of stage and screen
Weddings	Wedding Receptions are a speciality
Other associations	La Trattoria steak bar in Fish Street is part of the Prince Rupert Hotel

THE PRINCE RUPERT HOTEL HISTORY

The Prince Rupert Hotel, in Church Street, was opened as part of an ancient timber-framed building called Jones' Mansion in the 1950s. The mansion, dating from the early 17th century, was built by Thomas Jones, a lawyer, who was bailiff of Shrewsbury on six occasions. He became the first Mayor of the town in 1638. After his death his nephew, also called Thomas Jones, occupied the mansion. He was also a lawyer who later became Lord Chief Justice of Common Pleas.

The Hotel takes its name from Prince Rupert of the Rhine, a nephew of King Charles. He stayed there during the Civil War when he visited Shrewsbury to raise troops for the Royalist cause. At one time the mansion had a large forecourt, on the corner of St. Mary's Street and Church Street, which was built over in the eighteenth century. By the end of the nineteenth century after experiencing dwindling fortune the mansion had been divided into five houses.

The owners of the Prince Rupert later acquired the Central Hotel in Butcher Row, which stood on the site of the main entrance to the present hotel. Until about 1900 the building was a private dwelling but was converted into a temperance hotel by Mrs Elizabeth Jones. The hotel was taken over by the Smith family in the 1920s and for a while Albert Smith also ran a dairy from there. It remained a temperance hotel right up to the 1950s.

In 1960 the hotels were advertised: *"The Prince Rupert Hotel is a 15th century building. The Central Hotel, which is nearby, has been completely modernised. Both hotels offer the greatest comfort at very reasonable charges. Television Lounge. – There is hot and cold water, central heating, electric fires, and spring interior or Dunlopillo mattresses in every room. The hotels are in the very centre of the town in picturesque quiet side streets. The Prince Rupert Restaurant offers meals every day until 11 p.m. With first class cuisine and table license."*

The resident proprietors were Mr & Mrs Victor Hendel who were largely responsible for amalgamating and upgrading the two hotels. After Victor Hendel retired the hotel was bought by Len Morris-Jones an ex-lecturer at Shrewsbury Technical College who continued to improve the hotel's facilities making it one of the finest in the town. In recent years this comfortable and high-class hotel has catered for such personalities as George C. Scott, Edward Woodward and Susannah York who stayed there while filming "A Christmas Carol" in 1984. Other notable guests have included Richard Burton, Margaret Thatcher, Edward Heath and even Monica Lewinsky who was in town to publicise her autobiography.

Photo: The Prince Rupert Hotel Church Street c1955

THE BULL c.1624

A recently refurbished traditional town centre pub offering a good range of beers and lagers. Very good value home cooked food.

Theme	Refurbished historic town centre pub
Opening Hours	Mon - Sat 11 – 11 Sun 12 - 10.30
Licensee	Mark Glennister & Paul Desouza
Address	Butcher Row, Shrewsbury, Shropshire, SY1 1UW
Contact	T. 01743 344728
Brewery	Union Pub Company
House Beers	Banks's Bitter and Mild, Marstons's, Pedigree, HSB, Fosters + Extra Cold, Carlsberg + Extra Cold Marston's Full Cream,
Real Ales	No
Food	Home cooked food available from 5pm -9pm
Wine & spirits	Shocks, Archers, Bacardi.
Promotions	Meals 2 for the price of 1.
Entertainment	See comment
Accommodation	Recently refurbished 3 Double Rooms 2 ensuite, 1 four poster bed.
Awards	None
Customers	A good mix of regulars of all ages with many visitors
Comments	Planned live music will add to the atmosphere.

THE BULL`S HISTORY

Throughout its history this street has been the centre of the butcher's trade in Shrewsbury. At one time it was known as the Flesh Shambles, then as Double Butcher Row, to distinguish it from Single Butcher Row on Pride Hill, and finally by its present name. Until the 19th century animals were still being slaughtered in this street; very unpleasant for the inhabitants, especially on hot summer's days. Butchery must have been a very thirsty business as at one time six public houses with such names as the Tankerville Arms, the Lamb, the Rising Sun, the Cock and the Butcher's Arms once stood in this street.

The Bull is the last surviving inn on the row and the name can be linked with the street for nearly four hundred years. In St. Alkmund's Parish Register the inn is mentioned as early as 1624 and again in 1645. An old indenture dated 1653 refers to "a house called the Bull in a street called the Butchers Roe in Shrewsbury." It is also appears in the Corporation rentals in 1657.

Photo: The Bull Butcher Row 1960

Whether the earlier inn was on the site of the present Bull is unknown. The current premises date from around 1800 and were first recorded as a pub in 1868.

In 1900 the owner and landlord was George Edwards who had lived at the inn for twenty years. The inn comprised nine rooms - five private and four public with overnight accommodation for six visitors in three bedrooms. There were no stabling facilities but up an alley to the right of the inn was Bull Passage, which led to five houses. The passageway has since been incorporated into the inn.

When the Bull in Abbey Foregate closed in 1937 its sign, featuring the prize bull "Commandant" was hung at the Bull in Butcher Row. The work of local artist, Edwin Cole, the sign then adorned the front of this inn for many years.

From around 1938 until the late 1970s the Bull was run by the Kemmy Family, first by Patrick and then by his son Bill.

OWENS WINE BAR c. 2000

A modern brasserie and wine bar with plenty of live entertainment good food and real ale. Good fare all day starting with breakfast, coffee, lunch, afternoon tea and an evening meal with a good chance of some lively entertainment.

Theme	Continental Brasserie & Cocktail Wine Bar
Opening Hours	Mon – Sun 9-00 to11-00
Licensee	Pat Lever & Pedro Widmar
Address	Butcher Row, Shrewsbury
Contact	T. 01743 363 633
Brewery	Free house
House Beers	Leffe, Staropramen, Hoegaarden, Fransizkaner
Real Ales	Hobson's and Enville White
Food	Excellent Brasserie style food all day
Wines	Tanners – Continental
Promotions	None
Entertainment	Regular Music nights – Salsa night is Tuesday.
Accommodation	None
Awards	None
Customers	All ages and interests!
Comment	Excellent modern Cafe style venue with outside seating and very good food.

OWENS WINE BAR HISTORY

The wine bar is situated in a modern building in the middle of the historic Butcher Row. The site was once occupied by several houses, which included the Rising Sun an inn that had closed by 1906. At the rear was the Old Court, which contained several small cottages in cramped conditions. Towards the middle of the twentieth century the area was demolished and Richard Maddox, who owned a large store on Pride Hill and High Street, redeveloped the site into a warehouse and loading bay. The firm of Owen Owen bought Maddox Store in the 1970s and after they closed the present building was erected on the site.

Photo: Maddox Warehouse Butcher Row c.1960

THE THREE FISHES c.1780

A traditional public house set in the heart of the cobbled streets of Shrewsbury. It was the first pub in town to declare a smoke free atmosphere.

Theme	Traditional town centre pub.
Opening Hours	Mon-Sun12-2.15pm Full Menu available Mon - Sat 6- 8.30pm
Licensee	David Moss & Victoria Shutt
Address	Fish Street, Shrewsbury, Shropshire, SY1 1UR
Contact	T. 01743 344793 F. 01743 344793
Brewery	The Pub Company
House Beers	All real ales!
Real Ales	Fullers London Pride, Taylor's Landlord + Changing Guests
Food	Freshly prepared home cooked food.
Wine	From Tanners award winning local wine importers and merchants.
Promotions	None
Entertainment	None
Accommodation	None
Awards	Several Cask Mark Awards. Regularly features in the Good Beer Guide and was the West Shropshire CAMRA Pub of the year in 2002/03. Listed again in 2005 this record of consistency takes some beating and one of the few pubs to have won the pub of the year twice.
Customers	Any one who likes a good pint and good food
Comments	Consistent good quality for many years and the bonus of a smoke free environment since 1995

THE THREE FISHES' HISTORY

The inn was first known as the Fishes, then the Old Three Fishes and from 1838 to the present day as the Three Fishes. There are two possibilities for the origin of its name. The first, that it took its name from the emblem of the Abbott of Lilleshall Abbey who had a house at the junction of Fish Street and Butcher Row. The second, and more likely, is that the name reflects the fishmonger's trade carried out on boards hung on the wall opposite the inn. The fish market was held there on certain days of the week up until 1869 when it was removed to the new market hall at the top of Mardol.

The Three Fishes is a picturesque half-timbered building, with a jettied upper storey and probably dates from the 16th century. It was officially licensed in 1780 and was one of four inns recorded in the street, the others being the Half Moon, the Plough, and the Bear.

In 1831 the Salopian Journal informed its readers that John Birch at the Fishes House in Fish Street would hold a sale on Saturday 26th March at 5p.m. *"All that Free Hold Messuage or dwelling house situated in Fish Street and late in the occupation of Mrs Edwards deceased"*. At the beginning of the 1880s the landlord was Samuel Wilson Smith. In 1886 he changed the name to Ye Sportsman Inn but the new name proved unpopular and it soon reverted back to the old one.

Photo: The Three Fishes Fish Street c. 1930

By 1900 the Three Fishes was a tied house owned by Southam's Brewery who had their main works in Chester Street, now the site of the Gateway Education Centre. The landlord at the time, John Evans, was obliged to sell the brewery's beer and stout, but was allowed to make his own arrangements as to wines and spirits. The house had eight rooms, four private and four public. There were beds for eight paying guests, in three bedrooms, and there was a bagatelle board in the bar to entertain customers.

In 1995 it was the first public house in Shrewsbury to introduce a no smoking policy on its premises.

Nigel's Notes: At the time of writing May 2005 the effects of the no smoking rules in Irish pubs has had a dramatic effect with over 200 rural pubs closing so far. In spite of the expected changes to the law in England during 2008, some of the pub chains are thinking of introducing a ban well before the legislation takes effect.

THE NAGS HEAD pre 1780

A historic beer house without the benefit of a recent refurbishment, but with the most important quality, excellent beer. This is one of the most interesting of Shrewsbury`s timber frame buildings dating from 1421with superb exposed timbers which can best be viewed from the beer garden at the rear.

Theme	A historic building within an historic setting providing a service going back for centuries.
Opening Hours	Mon – Sat 12.00 – 11.00
Licensee	Russell Preece
Address	22 Wyle Cop, Shrewsbury, Shropshire, SY1 1XB
Contact	T. 01743 362455
Brewery	Punch Taverns
House Beers	Ansells Mild, Bass, Timothy Taylor Landlords, Robinsons Unicorn, Greene King IPA , Jennings Cumberland, Adnams Best,
Real Ales	Bass, Taylor's, Greene King,
Food	Baps & snacks
Wine	From Tanners award winning local wine importers and merchants.
Promotions	None
Entertainment	Juke Box, T.V.
Accommodation	None
Awards	None
Customers	Regulars are a cross section of Shrewsbury Society. The preferred watering hole for both mature and young people who enjoy the excellent beers and good company.
Comments	If you appreciate a traditional pint of quality ale and do not demand carpet on the floor, this pub should be on your visit list, don't miss the timber frame in the yard.

THE NAGS HEAD'S HISTORY

The Nags Head has been in existence since before 1780 and throughout its long history has kept the same name. It's housed in a timber-framed building, parts of which date from 1421. The top storey is jettied and projects several feet over the second floor. However like many buildings in town the over hang from the second storey has been masked by an extension of the ground floor. An old cupboard, in the front room at the

34

top of the house, has an unusual oil painting inside the door. It depicts a man carrying a trident, and is thought to be an illustration of Neptune.

At the rear of the inn is a fragment of Nag's Head Hall, once a house of quality and of a similar date to the inn. All that remains is a service area to the main hall, which contains a spere truss, a screens passage and three nicely carved doorways. The area behind the inn was known as Nag's Head Court and in the 1880s it contained seven houses.

The owner and landlord of the Nag's Head in 1882 was Alfred Timbs who advertised in a local directory, "Wines and spirits of first class quality." By 1900 the inn was owned by George Jones Holt, a brandy and wine importer, a wholesale dealer, and a bonder of spirits. He was an agent for Messrs Combe's London Stout and Porter and also Burton's India, Pale, Mild and Strong Ales.

Mr. Holt was mayor of Shrewsbury in 1891; and his grandson, Sir John Langford-Holt, was a Member of Parliament for Shrewsbury from 1945 to 1983.
At the beginning of the 20th century the landlord was John Stubb Woolrich whose customers were described as "good". The inn at this time consisted of five private and four public rooms.

Photo: the Nags Head c.1890

THE LION HOTEL

A larger town centre hotel with 59 rooms, including honeymoon suite, restaurant and bar. Open fires in winter.

Theme   An historic site owned by a modern hotel chain

Opening Hours   Usual hotel rules open all hours

Licensee   Kate Jordan

Address   Wyle Cop, Shrewsbury, Shropshire SY1 1UY

Contact   08706096167

Brewery/Owner Corus Hotels

House Beers   Bass, Boddingtons, XXXX

Real Ales   None

Food   Three star restaurant

Wines   International Selection

Promotions   Weekend breaks and meal offers.

Entertainment   A popular venue for the Shropshire Music Trust and Salsa every month in the Adam-style ballroom. With jive classes each week and regular exhibitions there is always something happening.

Accommodation 59 bedrooms

Awards   None

Customers   A wide cross section who enjoy the traditional values. Another popular wedding reception venue.

Comment   A great place to socialise.

THE LION HOTELS' HISTORY

Photo: The Lion Hotel Wyle Cop c. 1940

There are records of the Lion Hotel dating back to 1618 although its history stretches back further than that as it was built on one of the busiest roads leading in and out of Shrewsbury. The hotel is now housed in three buildings. The timber-framed section in the middle is the oldest with parts dating back to the 15th century. The top section was altered after the arrival of Robert Lawrence and most of the work including the beautiful Adam-style ballroom and assembly room are attributed to local architect Thomas Farnolls Pritchard.

The carved lions that stand over the front door and the assembly room at the rear are the work of another Shrewsbury man, John Nelson and are thought to date from 1777. The lower section of the hotel has been a private house and an Inland Revenue office, before being absorbed into the Lion.

With the arrival of Mr. Lawrence and the creation of the Assembly Room Shrewsbury and the Lion Hotel became the centre of social life for the nobility and local gentry who would attend dinners, concerts and glittering balls in the splendid surroundings of the hotel. The hotel's popularity continued throughout the 19th century with great artists and personalities, such as Paganini the violinist, Jenny Lind the Swedish Nightingale and Charles Dickens the novelist, all playing to huge audiences. Dickens who also stayed in the hotel wrote that he was lodged in "the strangest little rooms, the ceilings of which I can touch with my hand." He also commented that he could walk out onto a balcony and "lean over a queer old rail and look all down hill and slantwise at the strangest black and white houses, all of many shapes except straight shapes."

The Lion's reputation continued into the 20th century with many events being staged there including the fashionable dinner and dances that were so popular in the 1950s and 60s and the Saturday night dances organised by Bert Dann, where you could dance the night away to the music of Don Gilbert and his band.

As well as redeveloping the hotel into a fashionable social centre Lawrence also established the Lion as one of the principal coaching hotels in the country and was instrumental in changing people's minds on the route of the London to Holyhead road bringing it through Shrewsbury instead of Chester. Lawrence died in 1806 before reaping the full benefits of his work but within thirty years of his death twenty-three coaches travelled into town with over half of them using the Lion. One of the great spectacles of the town in the 1820s was the return of the Wonder Coach, driven by Samuel Haywood that travelled from London to Shrewsbury in sixteen hours. Haywood was never more than fifteen minutes late and crowds would gather at the top of the Cop, which was much narrower in those days to watch him gallop at full speed up the hill. As he reached the summit and without slacking speed he would do a sharp left hand turn into the Lion yard. The entrance gave him about six inches of clearance on either side with very little head room, but he accomplished this for over fifteen years without the slightest accident.

By 1900, with the coming of the railway the coaching trade became a thing of the past. The owner at this time was John Southern who ran a free house with sixteen bedrooms for the accommodation of nineteen guests. There were also five public rooms and stabling for thirty horses at the rear.

Many notable people have been accommodated at the Hotel including Thomas De Quincey who was lodged in the ballroom as all the other rooms were taken and Benjamin Disraeli who was the town's M.P. from 1841 to 1843. In 1855 after a short stay the novelist Nathaniel Hawthorne wrote that the hotel was "very dark in the lower apartments, pervaded with a musty odour, but provided with a white-neck-clothed waiter, who spares no ceremony in serving the joints of mutton."

37

THE LION AND PHEASANT

A pleasant privately owned and run hotel close to the English Bridge offering traditional facilities and service.

Theme   A comfortable privately run hotel

Opening Hours   Mon- Sat 12-2pm Sun 12-4pm

Licensee   Susan Howell

Address   49-50 Wyle Cop, Shrewsbury, SY1 1XJ

Contact   T 01743 236 288 F.01743 244 475

                        www.lionandpheasant.co.uk,

Brewery/owner   Free house - Mrs Chidlow

House Beers   A variety on offer including guests

Real Ales   London Pride

Food   Bistro and restaurant are open daily.

Wines   Worldwide Choice

Promotions   3 day weekend breaks

Entertainment   None

Accommodation 27 bedrooms offering en-suite or bath clock radio TV and tea/coffee making facilities. The popular Sunday Lunch has two sittings and the hotel also has two meeting and function rooms for up to 24 persons.

Awards   None

Customers   Diners looking for a personal service in comfortable surroundings

Comment   A pleasant hotel with personal and traditional service

THE LION AND PHEASANT'S HISTORY

The earliest records of the Lion and Pheasant are from letters, the first dated February 27th 1707, to be left "with Mr. Benbow at ye Lyon and Pheasant" and the second dated April 5th 1714, which was "to be left at ye Lyon and Pheasant on ye Wile Cop." The first official record of the inn does not appear until1804. The inn is housed in a building with an early 18th century frontage but with a much earlier timber-framed section at the rear, which probably dates from the 16th century.

The name of the inn is very rare as the two animals are an unusual combination. The reason for this strange pairings is unknown but often two names came together when two different public houses were amalgamated. Another suggestion is that the inn was once known as the Lion and Cock a much commoner combination when it was believed that a white cock carried a crystal in its gizzard, which warded off danger from a lion. Another suggestion is that the lion has been substituted for a dog as the Dog and Pheasant is a much more common sporting sign, but if and why the substitution took place, no one knows.

Photo: The Lion and Pheasant Wyle Cop c.1950

In 1857 the last cockfight to be held in Shrewsbury took place at the Lion and Pheasant when around two hundred birds were taken to the inn for the "sporting" event. News of the event spread around the town bringing in a large audience ready to wager on each fight but word also reached the ear of the local police force who raided the inn and arrested the promoters, who were taken to court and fined.

Throughout the 19th century and into the 20th the Lion and Pheasant was one of the main inns on that side of town for carriers travelling to villages to the south and east of Shrewsbury. In 1886 it was the starting point for carriers to Atcham, Wroxeter and Eaton Constantine; Bayston Hill, Condover and Longnor, Cross Houses, Harnage and Cound, Evenwood, Pulverbatch, Hookagate and Longden, Smethcott and Stapleton, Dorrington and Picklescott. Up until the 1930s the Lion and Pheasant continued its link with the local villages as a number of country buses that replaced the horse-drawn carrier's cart started from outside the inn.

In 1883 the inn was occupied by Mrs Mary Thorpe who advertised "Wines and spirits of the finest quality. Good stabling and lockup coach houses." Three years later she advertised that "Visitors and commercial gentlemen will find first class accommodation, with every convenience at the above hotel." By 1900 the inn was owned by Allsop's Brewery. It had eleven private and three public rooms with accommodation for twelve people in three rooms and stabling at the rear for eighteen horses. It also advertised "plenty of good accommodation". In 1961 the inn closed and was shut for the next twenty-three years. It remained empty until 1984 when it was reopened by the Mayor of Shrewsbury Councillor Fred Jones. The new owners Mr. and Mrs Ernest Chidlow of Uffington had spent around seven years converting the old inn into a first class hotel with exposed beams, restaurant, conference facilities and parking. Two local tradesmen Dave Powell and Ken Ayres carried out a great deal of the conversion work.

THE HOP & FRIAR c.1868

Theme	A young persons and students venue with older regulars during the day.
Opening Hours	Mon-Sat 11.00 - 11.00 Sun 12.00 - 10.30
Licensee	Pauline Anderson
Address	St Julian's Friars, Shrewsbury
Contact	T. 01743 344 339
Brewery	Banks's
House Beers	Banks's beers, Marston's Pedigree
Real Ales	Occasional guest beers.
Food	Snacks and light bites
Wines	Hardy's Merlot & Chardonnay house wines
Promotions	Regular promotions
Entertainment	Live music – every Tuesday
Accommodation	None
Awards	None
Customers	Young at heart pub-goers with a liking for music.
Comments	Another lively venue for the younger generation.

THE HOP AND FRIAR HISTORY

Two public houses have been recorded in St. Julian's Friars; the first was the Vulcan that was described in 1894 as an extinct inn. The other was the Acorn that was officially recorded in 1868 but had been in operation for a number of years earlier. The inn was fairly small when it opened and was situated at number 6 St. Julian's Friars. It traded there under the same name until recently when the building was completely renovated and extended into the house next door and given the new name the Hop and Friar.

The new name is appropriate as monastic orders were well known for their skill in brewing and at one time the land would have been under the control of the nearby friary. The closeness of the friary was shown in March 1864 when a number of human bones were dug up in an adjoining garden and were thought to be the remains of the friars who lived there.

Photo: The Acorn St Julian's Friars 1960

The friars from which the area takes its name were from the order of Franciscans, followers of St. Francis of Assisi. They were also known as the Friars Minors or the Grey Friars from the colour of their habit. They came to Shrewsbury at the beginning of the 12th century and remained in the town until their house was dissolved by Henry VIII. The only section of the friary that remains standing has been incorporated into cottages on the bank of the river next to the footbridge. They are thought to be the remains of the refectory.

At the beginning of the 20th century the Acorn was owned and managed by Annie Johnson a relation of the first recorded owner and landlord George Johnson. The inn had four private and four public rooms but no accommodation for guests and no stabling. It was a free house and they were described as having a good class of customer.

Nigel's Notes: Ale the traditional drink does not contain hops which were introduced to England in the 15th century, although Henry VIII did not approve. Hopped beer became more popular and has several advantages over ale for the brewer; the same amount of malt will produce twice as much beer as ale, beer is safer as the brew is sterilised by boiling, hops are a preservative and help clear the brew and improve the head of the beer.

41

THE OLD LION TAP c.1868

A wonderfully historic building that was refurbished by Martin Eebles in 1990.
This is a pub for "young" people of all ages and sees a lot of activity most
evenings.

Theme	Town centre young people pub venue in the evening. Older regulars during the day
Opening Hours	Open very late! One of the first to apply for later hours.
Licensee	Alan Briscoe
Address	Barracks Passage, Off Wyle Cop, Shrewsbury, SY11XA
Contact	T. 01743 245522
Brewery	Free house
House Beers	Bass, London Pride, Worthington & Tetley ranges, Coors fine light, Guinness Extra cold, Carling , Grolsch, Strongbow.
Real Ales	Yes
Food	By special request
Wine	Small selection
Promotions	Various offers, check for details
Entertainment	Video Juke Box, Quiz & Fruit Machines, Two Pool Tables, Darts & Karaoke
Accommodation	No letting rooms. 2 Function Rooms with food available if booked in advance.
Awards	None
Customers	Wide range of customers of all ages who like a lively atmosphere.
Comments	A pleasant place for a drink during the day, in another very historic building. A place to experience a very lively evening.

THE OLD LION TAP HISTORY

The Lion Tap is situated up Barrack's Passage the last of four shuts leading from Wyle
Cop to Back Lane, which is now known as Belmont Bank. In the 18th century the
passage was called Elisha's Shut from the family who lived in a house at the mouth of
the passage at the Wyle Cop end. The Elisha family were wealthy lawyers who played
a significant roll in the affairs of Shrewsbury. Samuel Elisha became a burgess of the
town in 1707 and was made mayor in 1725. He was followed by his son Edward who
became a burgess in 1727 and served as mayor in1743 he also held the office of
steward of the corporation.

After the Elisha family moved the shut became known as Barracks Passage as at some point in its history troops are supposed to have been billeted in the area. For a short while it was known as Lion Tap Passage but soon reverted back to Barracks Passage. The inn is housed in a timber-framed building that was erected in about 1426. The building runs along the full length of the passage and although slightly older than Henry Tudor House that faces Wyle Cop, the two buildings are linked.

It was first recorded as an inn around 1868 and was a beer house attached to the Lion Hotel. Between 1879 and 1883 it was called the Trotting Horse before reverting back to its original name until it closed in 1925

Photo: The Lion Tap Barracks Passage 1880

At the beginning of the 20th century the owners were Trouncer's Brewery who were based in Longden Coleham. The landlord was Robert Weatherby who took charge in 1894. He was tied to selling the brewery's beer but was free to choose his own stock of spirits and stout. There were five private and three public rooms and accommodation for eight people in four double rooms and stabling for two horses. The only complaint was that it had one urinal, which was not on the premises but two doors away. The inn was closed for a number of years but towards the end of the last century it was revived and for a short time in the 1990s was called the Trotting Horse before changing back to the Lion Tap.

43

THE OLD POST OFFICE c.1804

A refurbished coaching pub that is unusual in retaining its coach yard as a pleasant outside seating area for both food and drink.

Theme	An historical building that has been refurbished and offering another lively night out.
Opening Hours	Mon – Sat 12.00 – 11.00 Sun 12.00-3.00 7.00- 10.30
Licensee	Paul Witts
Address	1Milk Street, Shrewsbury SY1 1SZ
Contact	T. 01743 236 019
	www.theoldpostofficepub.com
Brewery	Banks's
House Beers	Marstons, Pedigree Banks's, Traditional Carlsberg, Stella, Fosters, Guinness + Extra Cold
Real Ales	Marstons Pedigree
Food	Good range at reasonable price
Wine	Good international selection
Promotions	Happy Hour Mon- Fri 6pm-7pm on selected Lines
Entertainment	Live music, Outside Seating
Accommodation	7 Guest Rooms offering Single, Double/Twin and Family Rooms available. Rates include Bed & Breakfast & VAT
Awards	None
Customers	A wide range of customers
Comments	A grade 11 listed Tudor building offering a warm welcome and fully refurbished accommodation that retains its essential character and charm behind the modern surface.

THE OLD POST OFFICE'S HISTORY

The Old Post Office is the last of five public houses once licensed for trade in Milk Street. The others were the Angel, the Beehive, the Mug House and the Sun Tavern. First recorded in 1804 the Old Post Office has kept the same name ever since. It has nothing to do with the Royal Mail but refers to the inn's role as a posting house for horse drawn coaches - and as late as 1900 there was stabling for thirteen horses in its extensive yard.

For most of the 19th century it was the headquarters for several carriers, and in 1886 wagons to Lyth Hill, Condover, Ryton and Wheathall, still left the inn on Wednesdays and Saturdays.

The hotel is housed in a building up a passageway to the rear of Proude's Mansion, parts of which date back to 1467. The structure of the inn itself is thought to date from the end of the 16th century.

In 1886 the landlord of the inn was John Parry who was also a maltster and hop merchant, who ran this business from a building on the corner of Mill Road in Abbey Foregate.

In 1900 the inn was owned by S.W. Soames and consisted of twenty rooms, six of which were for public use. In one of the rooms was a billiard table for the use of the customers.

The landlord in 1897 was Austen Skinner who was taken to court on 22nd April that year for refusing to allow a constable on duty on to his licensed premises. He was found guilty, had his licence endorsed and was fined five pounds plus nine shillings costs. Skinner left shortly afterwards and was followed in quick succession by Thomas Cornes in 1897, Silvester Williams in 1898 and George Andrews in 1901.

Photo: The Old Post Office Milk Street 1950

The best-known and most respected landlord in the 20th century was Sam Powell who took charge in 1937 and remained there until his retirement in August 1965. Over the years he brightened up the entrance to the inn with baskets and tubs of flowers that won him many prizes in the Town of Flowers competition. In 1947 he was elected as Councillor for the Castle and Stone Ward and in 1959 he became an Alderman of the Council.

As well as being a local councillor, he was also very heavily involved in local sport. During the 1930s he was the trainer and masseur for Shrewsbury Town Football Club. He also coached athletes for inter county tournaments, ran a boxing club, and trained both weight lifters and gymnasts who entertained large crowds around the Midlands at carnivals and other social gatherings. During his long stay at the Old Post Office the inn took on a strong sporting theme; the walls were hung with photographs of local athletes, footballers and sportsmen from the past.

THE WHEATSHEAF c1780

A recently refurbished pub with a coffee shop with Waldons Patisserie special desserts available until 3pm. Also some outside seating on the wide pavement.

Theme	A relaxed bar and coffee shop.
Opening Hours	Mon - Sat 9.00 - 11.00 Sun 12.00 - 10.30
Licensee	James Calder
Address	High Street, Shrewsbury, Shropshire, SY1 1ST
Contact	T. 01743 272702
Brewery	Union Pub Company
House Beers	Banks's Bitter and regular guest beers including Empire and Old Roger.
Real Ales	No
Food	Light meals are available Monday to Saturday with specials and a Sunday roast.
Wine	A world wide choice of over 30 different wines to suit every taste
Promotions	None
Entertainment	Plasma TV for major sports coverage
Accommodation	None
Awards	Finalist in the Union Pub Company Wine Retailer of the year in 2004.
Customers	A wide range of locals and visitors of all ages and lifestyles.
Comments	A warm welcome to regulars and visitors is assured at this pleasant town bar. The food is from local suppliers and home cooked on the premises.

THE WHEATSHEAF'S HISTORY

The inn was first recorded as a public house in 1780 and has always been known as the Wheatsheaf or the Old Wheatsheaf to distinguish it from the Wheatsheaf Inn just eight doors away on Wyle Cop. This is a building which dates from the 17th century and until recently it was clad in a mock Victorian timber-frame, removed when the inn was completely renovated in 2003.

The inn was auctioned in September 1822, together with an adjoining house, which were both occupied by a Mr. Roberts.

In 1900 the inn was privately owned by James Sykes of Dale Street in Liverpool and the landlady was Mrs Emma Atkinson who took over from her husband Thomas and continued to run it until the 1920s. During this period the inn consisted of thirteen rooms, of which the public used eight. There was also accommodation for six people in three bedrooms and stabling for two horses.

The corner where it stands at the junction of High Street and Milk Street was recorded in the Mercer's book in 1811 as Crockett's Corner, probably after a former landlord of the inn.

Photo: The Wheatsheaf High Street 1905

47

THE GOLDEN CROSS HOTEL c.1495

One of the oldest public houses in Shrewsbury, a relaxed atmosphere, with a fine restaurant.

Theme	An historic building and perhaps the oldest inn in town still in use. It has become a very comfortable restaurant with a no smoking policy during times when meals are served.
Opening Hours	Mon - Sat 11.00-11.00 Sun 12.00 10.30
Licensee	Gareth & Theresa Reece
Contact	T. 01743 362507 F. 01743 362507 www.goldencrosshotel.co.uk
Brewery	Free house
House Beers	Hobsons & Salopian
Real Ales	Yes
Food	Food which is a little special with a guarantee of quality and reasonable prices.
Wine	A thoughtful selection with something to please all tastes.
Promotions	None
Entertainment	Live Music. Watch out for the special events which sell out very quickly.
Accommodation	Simple and wholesome accommodation with an emphasis on friendly service. Rooms are available and in process of continuous improvement.
Awards	Shropshire Star 5 Star rating
Customers	Broad range of customers who prefer quality to quantity.
Comments	If you are looking for excellent food and ambience this is currently one of the best places to eat in town.

THE GOLDEN CROSS'S HISTORY

The Golden Cross is reputed to be one of the oldest public houses in Shrewsbury and was once known as the "Sextry," a corruption of sacristy, the place where the sacristan of old St. Chad's Church would have kept the church plate and vestments. Until 1794 a covered passage over Princess Street connected the church to the inn. Although alterations have occurred over the years, much of the building dates back to the last quarter of the 15th century. From the beginning the house was used for entertaining and we are informed in the Bailiff's accounts for 1495 that "*13s-2d in wine was spent upon the King's gentlemen in Sextre.*"

During the Civil War a group of Royalists from the town regularly met there and were described by one of their number as *"a club of good fellowship,"* while a member of the opposite persuasion referred to them as "a knot of company seekers."

The inn was first recorded as the Golden Cross in 1780 and it has been a popular meeting place throughout its history. In the 19th century the landlord was Thomas Harris and he was particularly proud of his dinners provided daily *"for those who wished to be served at his house or at their own houses."* Perhaps the town's first take-a-way service! He also sold fresh poultry ready for dressing and prime sausages in season.

Photo: The Golden Cross Inn, Golden Cross Passage c. 1917

In 1900 the inn was owned by Worthington & Co. and had six private and four public rooms. The landlady at this time was Maria Seddon who later changed her name to Banning. She was obliged to sell the brewery's beer and stout, but could supply her own spirits.

In February 1962 Michael and Audrey O'Dwyer became tenants of the inn. Michael was a retired National Hunt jockey and the couple were popular hosts, remaining at the inn for many years. Within a few months of their tenancy a problem arose when a section of the public wanted an end to the "Men Only" bar, which had been a tradition at the Golden Cross for many years. When the locals heard that their sanctuary was to lose its status, seventy male customers signed as petition of protest, which was sent to the brewery by the landlord. A compromise was reached with the "Men Only" bar functioning on weekdays, but with the ladies being allowed in at weekends, a situation that continued for a number of years.

BAILEYS VENUE BAR c.1849

Baileys Venue Bar has been dramatically refurbished and is now a "party venue for any occasion".

Theme	A recently renovated and themed venue bar.
Opening Hours	12-00 - 12-00 seven days
Licensee	A. Bailey
Address	39 & 40 High Street, Shrewsbury.
Contact	T. 01743 260 943
	www.baileysbar.co.uk
Brewery	Tied on beer
House Beers	Worthington, Creamflow, Boddingtons, Stella Artois, Carling, Carling Extra Cold, Strongbow, Guinness, Hoegaarden
Real Ales	None
Food	"Pub grub"
Wine	House choice
Promotions	Happy hour 4-7
Entertainment	Live music, DJ, and karaoke, plasma screens, mood lighting, scene sets on the walls!
Accommodation	None
Awards	UK Bar of the Year 2004!
Customers	Mostly young people. Hectic at weekends!
Comments	" A party venue great for hen nights"

BAILEYS HISTORY

Baileys Venue Bar occupies 39 and 40 High Street and has been associated with the drinks industry for over a century. The inn was first licensed, as the Criterion at 40 High Street in 1879.The definition of the unusual name is that the Criterion is the standard by which a thing is judged, which means this was the inn by which all others would be judged.

In 1900 it was a tied house owned by Lassells and Sharman Brewery but run by landlord Thomas Watkins. The inn had six private and four public rooms and accommodation for four people in two rooms. They also had excellent toilet facilities for that period with three water closets and two urinals. For entertainment the customers could play bar billiards or have a game of shove halfpenny.

The inn was later taken over by Butlers Brewery until the lease expired and it closed for a number of years. The last landlord of the old public house was Arthur Sambrook who moved to the Six Bells in Ditherington. His wife had fond memories of the old inn and remembered it had *"a cosy atmosphere and was a real old fashioned pub."*

The inn was closed for around eighteen months and was extended into the building next door, which had been occupied by C.H. Christmas who sold glass and china and sportswear.

Photo: The Criterion High Street c 1960

When the Criterion reopened it had been transformed into a Berni Inn steak bar that was run for many years by the Sidoli family. Later Honeycombe Leisure Ltd ran the inn as a restaurant before it was transformed into a theme bar, the Black Bull In Paradise in 1998.

In 2004 the bar was re-furbished, and opened as Baileys Venue Bar

Nigel's Notes: Over the last few years Shrewsbury has become a place where hen parties want to come to for the weekend and is perceived as a safe UK venue for such activities. A number of the historic pubs are catering for large parties and the pre night club evening trade whilst catering for their more traditional regulars during the day.

In this volume we have not attempted to cover the nightclubs and some hotels that have bar facilities that cater more for residents than general public.

THE HOLE IN THE WALL c1527

A popular venue bar set in an ancient building offering value for money for the traditional pub-goer.

Theme   A traditional town centre pub during the day. At night a young people's bar

Opening Hours   Mon – Sat 11.00 – 11.00 Sun 12.00 – 10.30

Licensee   Kay Clocherty

Address   1 Shoplatch Shrewsbury SY1 1HF

Contact   T. 01743 264971

Brewery   M & B

House Beers   Banks's, Worthington

Real Ales   Bass

Food   Standard Pub Grub

Wine   Brewery choice with offers on full bottles

Promotions   Meals 2 for £5.95 Wens and Sun

Entertainment   TV and live DJs on 5 nights

Accommodation None

Awards   None

Customers   Daytime a wide variety evenings young people

Comments   Good value and meals with large portions.

THE HOLE IN THE WALL'S HISTORY

The inn that we have today is an amalgamation of two former public houses, the Market Vaults and the old Hole In the Wall. The inn is also on the site of a much older hostelry the Gullet Inn, which was mentioned in accounts for the town as early as 1527. For almost two hundred years it seems to have been the favourite lodgings for travelling performers, which we see from the same accounts when Lord Willoughby's actors, who were staying at the Gullet, were rewarded by the town council with 3s 1?d for their performance. In 1630 there is also mention of the inn having its own indoor tennis court for Real Tennis as played by Henry VIII. The inn was sold in 1788 and was closed by 1793.

Photo: The Market Vaults   c.1926

The section of the inn that faces Shoplatch and runs into the Gullet Passage has the date of 1863 embellished across the front of the building. It was first recorded as the Market House in 1868 the year before Shrewsbury's new general market was opened on the opposite side of the road. It has been called the Market or the Market Vaults but to the locals it was also known as the Blood Tub. There has been some speculation about the origin of this name, with some believing that it referred to the colour and texture of the beer, while others thought that it was once a good place for a brawl.

W.R. Gough the manager in 1886 advertised *"Wholesale and retail wine and spirits, ale and porter dealer. Burton Ale with Dublin Stout on draught and in bottles. First class spirits and cigar Billiards and smoke rooms.* In 1900 the inn was owned by William Hall the proprietor of the Tithe Barn Street Brewery in Preston. The landlord was James Cave who ran a free house with seven private and four public rooms and overnight accommodation for two people in single rooms.

A fire broke out at the inn in December 1943 when Laurie Miller was landlord. A wooden floor became alight but with the rapid arrival of the National Fire Brigade, who were based close by on Cross Hill, the blaze was soon extinguished with little damage to the inn.

The old Hole in the Wall stood in Drayton's Passage a narrow alley leading from Shoplatch. Its name was derived from its location in a confined space and was originally the local nickname for the inn. It was first recorded in 1883 as the Star Vaults and later as Hughes's Wine and Spirits Vault. It is built on the site of Shute's Place a 13th century stone mansion and in the 17th century the cellar was part of a debtor's prison.

In 1985 a plan costing over £250,000 to incorporate the two inns was unveiled by the brewery Mitchell and Butler. Work took several months to complete and several remains from the old mansion were uncovered and incorporated into the new inn. Several exciting finds were also unearthed including clay pipes, pottery and a letter about the Black Death dated 1660. The first landlord of the refurbished inn was Eric Rock with his wife Agnes who had been licensees of the Monkmoor Hotel since 1980.

ADMIRAL BENBOW c.1835

A traditional English pub for the mature customers seeking real ales from local breweries with pleasant outside seating.

Theme | A traditional pub with excellent beers.

Opening Hours | Mon-Wed 5.00-11.00 Thurs-Sat 12-2.30 & 5.00-11.00 Sun 7.00-10.30

Licensee | Claire Noakes & Mike Vaughan

Address | 24 Swan Hill, Shrewsbury, Shropshire, SY1 1NF

Contact | T. 01743 244423

Brewery | Free House – CAMRA meet there!

House Beers | Always at least 6 local brewery's products including 6 Bells Cloud Nine - 3Tuns Castle Steamer - Salopian Golden Thread & Heavensent. Draft Guinness, Carling, Stella Artois, Ciders on draft Strongbow & Renshaws

Real Ales | Yes, always at least six on tap

Food | None

Wines | Extensive selection and independent choice. Good Selection of Malt whiskies available

Promotions | None

Entertainment | Darts, quiet background music

Accommodation | None - Private function room available.

Awards | Cask Mark Award – CAMRA good beer guide.

Customers | Mature drinkers over 30 years old looking for a town centre pub with quality real ale.

Comments | An excellent award winning pint in a pub convenient to the centre of town.

ADMIRAL BENBOW'S HISTORY

The inn was first recorded in 1835 as the Talbot Tap, which was probably connected to the Talbot Hotel in Market Street. It was a beer house where the coachmen and servants of the wealthier classes would stay while their masters and mistresses were being entertained in the grander surroundings of the hotel. A Talbot was a dog and is an emblem on the arms of the Earls of Shrewsbury, whose family name was Talbot.

The inn was first recorded as the Admiral Benbow in1861 around ten years after the hotel closed. It commemorates Shrewsbury's greatest navel commander Admiral John

Benbow, the son of a local tanner, who was born in a house on Coton Hill around 1650. Part of the house remained in Furrows Garage until the building was demolished in 2004. In a glass-fronted case on the side of the house was a section of a sycamore tree with a key hanging from a rusty old nail. It was supposed to have been put there by Benbow on the day he ran away to sea as a boy. William III called him "Honest Benbow" and he has become known as the Nelson of the 17th century.

He fought the French off Beachy Head in 1690 and at La Hague in 1692. His greatest battle was off the coast of Jamaica where he drove off a much larger French fleet after

some of his captains refused to fight. During the battle he was mortally wounded but his gallantry is recorded in a ballad that tells us that after having his legs removed by chain-shot, he remained in control of the battle by having his bed brought up onto the quarterdeck. His remains lie in St. Andrew's Church in Kingston Jamaica and in 1841 a beautiful marble monument was erected to his memory in St. Mary's Church after £60 was raised by a number of Shrewsbury residents.

In 1900 the brewers Brindley & Co of Burton-on-Trent owned the inn. The building, which dates from around 1800 had five private and four public rooms, there was also stabling at the rear for eleven horses.

During the last century the inn's most popular landlord was H. "Happy Sheldon" who moved from the Coach and Horses just two doors away in 1937 and was there until his death in 1957. In 1943 he displayed a potato on his bar that was in the shape of a "V" for victory that been dug up by one of his customers, Mr. Fred Williams, in his garden in Castlefields.

Photo: The Admiral Benbow Swan Hill c.1943

THE COACH AND HORSES c.1861

A traditional pub serving excellent real ales and draught beers and lagers, with a comfortable restaurant serving first-rate food, all week.

Theme	A comfortable traditional pub.
Opening Hours	Bar 11.00- 11.00 all week Sun 12.00 - 10.30
Restaurant	Weekdays 12.00 - 2.30 & 6.30 - 9.30 Sun 11.30 – 4.30
Licensee	Dean Morris & Jo Piggott
Address	Swan Hill, Shrewsbury, Shropshire, SY1 1NF
Contact	T. 01743 365661
	www.odleyinns.co.uk
Brewery	Odley Inns – free house
House Beers	Leffe Blonde, Hoegaarden, Staropramen, Arizona, Eccleshall Top Totty, Holdens XB, London Pride, Cider on draft, Ecclestones, and Olde English.
Real Ales	Yes – excellent selection.
Food	Has a wide reputation for good home cooked food.
Wines & Sprits	A choice of over a dozen Malt whiskies available.
Promotions	None
Entertainment	Acoustic live music
Accommodation	None
Awards	Town of Flowers awards for the magnificent Baskets on show.
Customers	A wide range from all walks of life and ages.
Comments	A welcoming traditional pub just off the main streets the local for many of the town centres residents. An excellent carvery with a good range of food lunchtimes and evenings.

THE COACH AND HORSES HISTORY

The Coach and Horses public house is an early 19th century building on the corner of Swan Hill and Cross Hill, it was first recorded in 1861. Previous to this the Swan Inn, which gave the road its name, stood on the opposite corner between 1780 and 1820. The inn has always been a popular meeting place and until fairly late in the last century had a "Men Only" bar.

In 1886 W. Bennett the landlord advertised that he was an agent for the brewer Richard Wilson who was an ale and porter bottler from Bridgnorth.

In 1900 the owners were Worthington & Co of Burton-on-Trent. Mrs Mary Davies was the landlady and the inn consisted of eight private and four public rooms with one urinal and water closet, which were described as "fair". There was no over night accommodation, stabling or entertainment for the drinkers.

Photo: The Coach and Horses c. 1955

In 1937 John Lewis took over as landlord from "Happy" Sheldon. Previously he had been landlord of the Hand and Diamond in Coedway and at the Cross Keys in Llanymynech. It was an association that was to last around half a century as the running of the inn was later taken over by his son Fred.

On Saturday morning 17th May 1962 a fire broke out in the upstairs sitting room causing a considerable amount of damage. Firemen fighting the blaze had to wear breathing apparatus to get to the seat of the fire but they were quickly on the scene as the town's fire station was only twenty yards away and they knew the premises well as several of them were regular drinkers at the inn.

Photo: Inside The Coach & Horses with Fred and Alma Lewis 1974

Nigel's Notes: During the late 1980`s the inn was modernised and extended down Cross Hill by Roger Goodall who developed the business from wet sales to a successful restaurant for lunch. Roger could down a pint in 3 seconds and is a practical joker who also has enough charm to cut a customers tie off just below the knot for fun. Roger also previously owned a Hand and Diamond the one near Loton Park before coming to "The Coach."

THE EXCHANGE c.1800

Eclectic traditional pub turned disco music bar. In the evening not the best place to go to have a quiet conversation!

Theme	A mixed pub in the daytime, and a music bar at night
Opening Hours	Mon Closed Tues 7 - 11 W,T,F,S.12-00 - 11.00 Sunday 7 - 10.30
Licensee	Gaynor & Mark Latham-Chadwick
Address	Bellstone, Barker St., Shrewsbury, SY1 1HU
Contact	T. 01743 362481
	www.theexchangeonline.co.uk
Brewery	Scottish & Newcastle
House Beers	Hand pulls - Directors, Ruddles John Smiths, Draft Guinness, Fosters, 1664, Becks, Draft Cider Strongbow.
Real Ales	No
Food	No
Wine & Spirits	Vodka Bar, Cocktails Shots and Shooters.
Promotions	Weds & Thurs Bottles two for price of one. Double Vodka & DT £1.49 - Red Rooster £1.79
Entertainment	Disco music throughout the week
Accommodation	No letting rooms – available for private functions
Awards	One of the strictest run young people pubs in town!
Customers	"Crumblies to trendies" depending on the day and hour!
Comments	During the day an ideal place for a light refreshment including tea or coffee that is handy for the market.
	In the evening expect a lively start, with music from the surround sound system and youngsters of all ages, on the way to the riverside nightclubs.

THE EXCHANGE'S HISTORY

The address of the old Exchange varied between St. John's Hill and Bellstone as the front door of the building straddled the corner of both streets. The original inn was housed in a building that dated from around 1800. It was first recorded in 1868 and was famous for its stout and oyster bar. In 1900 the ownership of the inn belonged to the Watton Estate, the trustees being Robert Watkins of the Shrewsbury Chronicle and V.C.L. Crump of Town Walls. Mr. Watkins' house and both the Chronicle Office and print works were only a few yards away on St. John's Hill.

The old inn consisted of seven private and five public rooms with overnight accommodation for eight people in four double rooms. There was one good water closet and urinal. The customers were described as working class but well behaved. Wilderspools Brewery provided the supply of ales and beer.

During the 1930s the Borough Council embarked on a scheme to provide an inner ring road and to add more car parking space in this area of town. Many buildings were demolished in Bridge Street and Barker Street and so was the whole west side of Bellstone, from Claremont Hill to St. John's Hill, including the old Exchange.

However before the old Exchange was dismantled a new inn was built at the rear so that there would be no interference with trade when the old building was knocked down.

The last licensees of the old Exchange were Mr. and Mrs Jack Dixon who were in charge during the move in to the new building on 30th September 1935.

Mrs Dixon remembered that the new Exchange took around eighteen months to build and the brewery bought the property next-door so they could build a much bigger hostelry. They entered the licensed trade in December 1933 and after the death of her husband in 1945 Mrs Olive Dixon continued to successfully run the inn until the 1980's. She was always a popular figure and was President of the Salop Licensed Victuallers' Auxiliary Association in 1956. She was also very proud of the floral displays that decorated the front of the Exchange during the summer, which won her a number of prizes in the Town of Flowers Competition.

Photo: The Exchange Bellstone c.1900

THE BELLSTONE c.2000

A recently opened town centre brasserie and hotel with excellent food.

Theme	A meeting place with quiet refined comfort.
Opening Hours	Mon – Sat 8-30 - 11-00 Sun - 9-30 – 10-30
Licensee	Nigel Lee
Address	Bellstone, Shrewsbury
Contact	T. 01743 242 100
	www.bellstone-hotel.co.uk
Brewery	Free
House Beers	Boddingtons, Flowers IPA, XXXX, Stella, Staropramen
Real Ales	None
Food	Wide choice of snacks and main meals of consistently high quality.
Wines	Addisons of Newport
Promotions	None
Entertainment	None – a novelty to be able to converse!
Accommodation	18 en suite lodge-style double and twin rooms.
Awards	None
Customers	All who enjoy an informal place to meet and eat with an excellent standard of food and drink.
Comment	Warm welcome from some of the smartest staff in town.

THE BELLSTONE HISTORY

When the new inner loop road was put through in the 1930s a number of Georgian houses had to be demolished or rebuilt on a new line. The two buildings on either side of Claremont Hill were demolished but rebuilt in a sympathetic style. The last person to occupy the site before demolition was Mrs Rosina Barton a tobacconist. After the road had been widened and redeveloped the Little Fruit Market was opened on the corner by S. J. Richards. By 1955 he was also running a similar business on Wyle Cop and had a warehouse in the vaults of the old market hall. The shop closed in the 1960s and Sidoli's extended their business into the building transforming it into a cafe and ice-cream parlour. At the beginning of the new millennium the building changed hands again becoming an upmarket restaurant and small hotel.

Photo : the Little Fruit Market c1955

ROWLEYS c.1780

A recently refurbished town centre pub opposite Rowley's Mansion. A combination of a wine and sports bar!

Theme	A sports and theme bar.
Opening Hours	Mon - Wed 10 - 11. Thurs - Sat 10 - 12 Sun 12.00 - 10.30
Licensee	Glenda Pugh
Address	Barker Street, Shrewsbury
Contact	T. 01743 246496
Brewery	Banks's
House Beers	Banks's & guests, Mansfield Smooth, Fosters & cold, Carlsberg & cold, Guinness & cold, Hoegaarden, Starhoven, Strongbow and Woodpecker.
Real Ales	None
Food	Pub Grub served Mon – Sat 10.00 – 16.00
Wines & Spirits	Bottles Cocktails and shooters
Promotions	Various special promotions
Entertainment	Disco music & big screen sport
Accommodation	None
Awards	None known
Customers	Young people of all ages
Comments	An entertaining place. Clubbers meet here on the way to the nightclubs close by. Major sports events can be viewed on the plasma screens. Live music, DJ's and Funk nights on Fridays.

ROWLEYS HISTORY

This inn has had several changes of name during its long history. It was first recorded as the Slipper in 1780, the Hope and Anchor between 1828 and 1835, and the Oddfellow's Arms from 1851 to 1856. However it had reverted back to being the Old Slipper Inn by 1868.

The old inn stood in front of the present building but was demolished in the 1930s to widen Barker Street. In 1900 the old inn consisted of twelve rooms, seven private and five for public use. There was also overnight accommodation for six people in two bedrooms. The owner and landlord was John Palmer who was reported to be a well-organised man who managed his business well. He had a good outdoor trade and his customers were mainly the residents of Barker Street, which at this time was densely populated. In Court One that ran to the side and rear of the inn there were ten houses packed into a very cramped area.

Photo The Slipper Barker Street c.1936

The new inn was opened in 1939 and was reported to have a fine sign over the door showing a man known as the "Slipper" unleashing a greyhound at a hare-coursing match. Unfortunately by the 1970s this had been replaced by one depicting an oriental type shoe with a large pompom on the toe!

In recent years the inn has changed its name as many times as it has changed its image. In the mid 1990s it closed for refurbishment and was re-opened in 1998 as Jackson's. In 2002 it was renamed the Merchant Stores and remained so until the end of 2004. In 2005 it was renamed Rowley's, taking its name from William Rowley the rich merchant who had built the fine timber-framed house and brick mansion across the road.

Nigels Notes:
William Rowley - House and Museum
William Rowley was one of the most significant brewers and maltsters in the history of the town. He was born in Worfield into a family of maltsters and brewers in 1572, by the age of 22 he had established himself in Shrewsbury and was appointed a Burgess of the town.

His business was probably based in the timber frame building known as Rowley's House which now is occupied by Shrewsbury Museum's Service. The evidence that this was a commercial building is that there are no chimneys or fireplace and a sack hoist is built into the roof timbers. The house behind the timber frame building is one of the first to be built of brick in Shrewsbury and remained in the family for several years before falling out of use.

Back in 1635 his business was described as "very vast brew house of Mr Rowley's, the brewing vessels wherein are capable of 100 measures" He took advantage of the growth of the Welsh cloth trade to move into Drapery and in 1634 and 1640 he was master of the Shrewsbury Drapers.

The building was rediscovered and saved from demolition by the then Borough Surveyor A.W. Ward in the 1930`s It was in use as a warehouse when purchased by the Borough in 1972.

LLOYDS IN THE TOWN c.1985

A town centre venue bar much frequented by young people. One of the first bars to have a late night music licence thus pre-empting the new licensing laws. In May 2005 the pub changed hands to new owners, Scottish & Newcastle

Theme	New theme anticipated following change
Opening Hours	Mon Thurs 12.00-3.00 7.00 - 11.00 Fri 12 – 3 7 -11
	Sat & Sun 12.00 – 12.00
Licensee	Theresa Dwyer
Address	Hills Lane, Shrewsbury. SY1 1QU
Contact	T. 01743 235837
Brewery	Scottish & Newcastle
House Beers	John Smiths, Fosters, Miller, Kronenberg, Guinness, Strongbow
Real Ales	No
Food	Basic bar menu
Wine	House wine
Promotions	Reduced prices on a wide range of beers. Draft and bottled House Wine at £5.45
Entertainment	Big Screen Sky Sports DJ Fri Sat Sun
Accommodation	None
Awards	None
Customers	Wide range during day, mainly young people in evening
Comments	Another lively pub with a mix of regulars during the day and more, but not exclusively young people at night.

LLOYDS HISTORY

Lloyds In The Town is a relatively new inn, opening in August 1985. Previous to this Richard Maddox & Co. who had a large departmental store in the centre of town had used the building as store. Before the building was taken over by Vincent Greenhous a local garage owner and he opened a subsidiary company there known as High Speed Tyres. He formed the company in 1935 and had branches at Shrewsbury, Hereford and Wrexham. The company specialised in the sale and repair of tyres. A re-treading plant was later installed at Shrewsbury.

Photo: Lloyds c.1950

The building lay empty for several years but was given a new lease of life after the new Victorian Arcade had been opened on the old Singleton & Cole's site between Mardol and Hill's Lane and the cottages on Hill's Lane had been refurbished.

There had been several public houses in the area but with the closure of the Green Dragon in the early 1970s it became a dry locality. An opportunity was seen and the old garage was transformed into a new inn called the Queen Victoria. The grand opening took place on the 22nd August 1985. The inn was a free house and the landlord and landlady of the new enterprise were Henri and Liz Quinn. Henry was very well known in the area as the manager of Park Lane the nightclub in Raven's Meadow. The couple then went on to own the Shrewsbury Hotel. The inn was opened at eight o'clock and for the first hour all drinks of spirits or beer were on sale at a penny a measure, but customers were warned that if they were not smartly dressed they might be refused admission. An advert for the inn recommended "The superbly relaxed atmosphere created by the luxurious carpets and seating, well complimented by the scattering of the old gas lamps and period paintings, thus creating the olde worlde atmosphere within this new modern concept." You could also enjoy a wide and varied menu, which included steaks, and traditional Victorian meals and you could step back in time and sample life as the Victorians did, with superb ales and a variety of good wines and spirits. The centrepiece of the new inn was the canopied fireplace with a painting of Queen Victoria in which the Monarch looked "clearly amused."

THE KINGS HEAD c.1404

This successful pub has been in the same family ownership for decades and offers traditional value. It is one of Shrewsbury's most historic buildings.

Theme   Traditional town centre pub

Opening Hours   Mon - Sat 10.30 - 11.00 Sun 12.00 - 10.30

Licensee   Edith Mary Aldridge

Address   48 Mardol, Shrewsbury, Shropshire, SY1 1PP

Contact   T. 01743 362843

Brewery   Punch Taverns

House Beers   Tetley Bitter, M & B Mild, Bass, Worthington, Guinness, Stella, Carling, Staropramen, Strongbow.

Real Ales   Bass

Food   Home cooked food freshly made from local produce.

Wine   House wines on optic

Promotions   Spirits are sold in the larger 35ml measures and a double 70ml is on offer at £3.20

Entertainment   None

Accommodation None available at present.

Awards   None

Customers   Range from 18 to 80 who enjoy a traditional pub with good beer and food.

Comments   A must visit for anyone interested in history. This is a superb timber frame building with the bonus of the mediaeval wall painting and well kept beer.

THE KINGS HEAD'S HISTORY

The original King's Head stood on the top corner of Roushill and Mardol in a building that was demolished for road widening in the 1960s. It was last used by Mr. Richard Bromley a seed merchant and a former mayor of Shrewsbury. This inn was known as the Last Inn but changed to its present name around 1804 when presumably the title was transferred at the time the former inn closed.

The inn is situated in one of the most attractive timber-framed houses in the town. It has been accurately dated to 1404 but has been altered many times during its history. At one time it had two roofs with gable ends and attic windows facing the street. Medieval tiles, thought to come from the Chapel of St. John that stood across the river in Frankwell, were once laid over the oak boards of an upper room. They were removed in the first half of the 20th century though some were saved and laid, as a border in the entrance hall but were lost during later alterations. During alterations carried out in 1962 workmen discovered several interesting finds including a priest's hole, part of which was being used as a broom cupboard, a bundle of sulphur matches, a scissor shaped candle trimmer and snuffer and several clay pipes. One interesting item was found when part of the lounge wall was removed. It was a letter in excellent condition and dated January 9th 1826. It was addressed to the landlord Mr. F. Griffith and was from a Mr. Ian Fransom of Pool Quay near Welshpool. In clear handwriting he asks the landlord, "Sir will you have the goodness to look at the head of the bed ware I slept. I left my watch thare. If you will have the goodness to take care of it for me and send me word whether it is safe."

For several months during 1987 the inn was completely refurbished by the brewery Mitchells and Butler. During the work an exciting discovery was made as workmen removed brickwork from the front of a ground floor fireplace to expose an older chimneybreast. There they found a wall painting hidden from view for several hundred years. It measures about six feet by six feet and depicts the scenes of the Last Supper and the Annunciation. The figures are well preserved and are thought to date from the late 14th to the early 15th century. Further artwork of a later date was found in a room on the second floor and is made up of two stencilled patterns.

During the 19th century the lower end of Mardol, Roushill and the Quay area was the "Red Light" part of the town and the "ladies of the night" often brought the landlords of the King's Head into conflict with the law. In February 1843 Thomas Downes was charged with "Suffering notorious bad characters to assemble in his house." P.C. Thomas informed the court that after hearing a great commotion at the inn around midnight, he entered and found about a dozen women entertaining around thirty men. The ladies left by the front door only to enter by the rear door after the police had left. When the police returned an hour later the party was still going on "fast and furious" and several of the women were arrested, taken to court and fined £1 plus 9s-6d costs.

In 1868 landlord James Newton was sent to prison for fourteen days, as he had no money to pay the £1 fine imposed for selling liquor during prohibited hours on a Sunday to five men and a prostitute. As late as July 1892 James Cockcroft was prosecuted for "permitting his licensed premises to be the habitual resort of reputed prostitutes." He was fined ten shillings, which included costs. The 1900 survey reveals that the inn had six private and three pubic rooms with overnight accommodation for eight people in two bedrooms. Mr. Cockcroft was still the owner and landlord and his customers were described as the labouring class and women.

Photo: The Kings Head Mardol c.1935

THE BEDROOM.

Theme   A young persons themed bar in the evening with locals and regulars
                 most times of the day.

Opening Hours   Mon Tues 12.00 – 11.00 Wens – Sat 12.00 – 12.00
                 Sun 12.00-10.30

Licensee   Nemanie Purslow

Address   49 Mardol Shrewsbury SY1 1PP

Contact   T. 01743 271568

Brewery   Spirit Group

House Beers   Tetley, Guinness, Carlsberg, Carling, Stella, Strongbow

Real Ales   None

Food   12.00 – 6.00 Basic pub grub

Wine   House wine

Promotions   Meals 2 for £4.95 Bottle House Wine £4.95

Entertainment   Big Screen Video Music Master
                 DJs Wens Thurs Fri Sat Sun

Accommodation None

Awards   None

Customers   Appeals to wide age range during day. Evening more young people

Comments   A special night out for party goers with hen parties a speciality

THE BEDROOM'S HISTORY

During its history the building has been put to many different uses and stands in a
Burgage plot that was established originally in Saxon times.

From around 1880 it was the home of John Yeomans a cabinet maker and upholsterer
who lived and worked there until about 1896. John Corbet Pickering who was listed as
an ironmonger, engineer and an agricultural implement maker, next occupied the shop.
He started his business around 1890 in Smithfield Road. Mr. Pickering continued his
business in Mardol and Smithfield Road until 1902 when trading ceased and he was not
mentioned in any of the town's directories until 1909 when he was listed as running a
butcher's shop at 56 Coton Hill.

In 1903 part of the building was being used by Simon Richards the Superintendent of
the Royal Fire Brigade, perhaps as a temporary fire station, as their old headquarters in
Mardol Head was being absorbed into the new offices of the Royal Insurance
Company. A butcher occupied the other part of the building by the name of H. Brookes.

By 1906 the building was occupied by Sydney Hubbard a green grocer and cycle agent, and by James Bray a mineral water manufacturer, who had also taken over the Smithfield Road site. Mr. Bray was the landlord of the Britannia Hotel in Mardol and he called his mineral water factory the Britannia Works. An advert for that period recommended his "High Class Aerated Water". He also bottled Burton ales and stout, Pilsner larger beer and Herefordshire cider, hop beer and stone beer.

In 1910 James Bray occupied part of the Mardol site while the other section was empty.

By 1913 Mr. Pickering was back in both the Mardol and Smithfield sites and was registered as a cycle and motorcycle agent and motor garage. During the second half of the 20th century the business moved away from motorised machines to concentrate on bicycles, accessories and toys. The shop was moved across the road to smaller premises in Mardol and Mr. Pickering finally stopped trading in December 2002. The business was run by three generations of the Pickering family, each with the same Christian names, John Corbett.

After Mr. Pickering had moved out of 49 Mardol the shop was transformed into a restaurant and cocktail bar called Muswells. It was known later as Butlers and then Porters before changing to the Pig and Truffle in the early 1990s, a name it kept until 2002 when it became the Bedroom.

Photo: J C Pickering Shop c.1960

YATES WINE BAR c 1879

Theme	A recently modernised pub.
Opening Hours	Mon – Sat 11.00 – 11.00 Sun 12.00 10.30
Licensee	Martina Fleming
Address	58 -59 Mardol, Shrewsbury, SY1 1PP
Contact	T.01743 343534
Brewery	Yates
House Beers	John Smiths & Worthington + 6 Lagers
Real Ales	None
Food	Available Mon – Thur 11.00-9.00 Fri-Sat 12.00 – 8.00 Sun 12.00 – 9.00 normal Yates fare.
Wine	House
Promotions	Regular Promotions Change Frequently
Entertainment	Pool & Plasma Screens Terrestrial Sports
Accommodation	None
Awards	None
Customers	Wide range during day, a young persons bar in the evening
Comments	A fairly new Yates Wine Bar!

YATES`S HISTORY

Yates Wine Lodge is housed in part of a building that used to be known as the Mardol Vaults. There were several inns in Mardol called Vaults and to stop confusion they were usually prefixed with the name of the landlord or owner. At number 50 Mardol there was Bulmer's Vaults named after the brewery, at number 69 Mardol there was Simpson's Vaults named after the landlord and number 76 Mardol was known as either Salisbury's or Makepeace's Vaults, again after two previous landlords. Yates Wine Lodge was first recorded in 1879 as the Wrexham Vaults. It changed its name to Morgan's Vaults in 1883 and to Mainwaring's Vaults in 1896 both after the landlord. It was first recorded as the Mardol Vaults from 1916 a name it kept until its closure, although at times it was known to the locals as Truman's Vaults after the owner and brewer who supplied the beer. The name Mardol is taken from the street it was situated in. An early interpretation of the name links it to the Welsh "mur" a wall and "dol" a meadow but another theory is that it is derived from the Anglo-Saxon "maere" a boundary and "deofol" the devil and means the devil's boundary. Before the inn closed it sported a fine sign outside depicting the devil crouched behind a boulder.   In 1900 the inn was owned by Truman, Hanbury, Buxton & Co. brewers from Burton-on-Trent. The house was tied to selling the brewery's beer but free to sell its own choice of wines and spirits, stout and bottled ale. There were nine private and two public rooms with overnight accommodation for six people in three double rooms. At the rear in Roushill there was stabling for three horses. On the 3rd February 1900 the landlord Walter Perry was in court for allowing drunkenness on his licensed premises. He was found guilty by the magistrates and fined £1, which included costs.

Photo: Mardol Vaults c.1926

THE SHREWSBURY HOTEL c1651

A pleasant hotel offering fine views of the River Severn

Theme	A JD Weatherspoon Hotel with a library/lounge feel.
Opening Hours	Hotel Hours
Licensee	
Address	Bridge Place, Mardol, Shrewsbury, SY1 1PU
Contact	T. 01743 236203 F. 01743 236197
	www.jdwetherspoon.co.uk
Brewery	J.D. Wetherspoon
House Beers	Full Wetherspoon's range of beers
Real Ales	Yes
Food	Wide range of budget meals.
Wine	Various house wines available
Promotions	See website for current specials
Accommodation	There are 22 rooms all of which have en-suite bathroom with tea/coffee making facilities, remote controlled TV with a computer modem point, telephone and hair driers.
Awards	None
Customers	Wetherspoon fans who like the value for money approach of the organisation.
Comments	Watch out for progress towards smoke free.

HISTORY OF THE SHREWSBURY HOTEL

This inn was first recorded as the Harp, or the Welsh Harp, and early records indicate that there was an inn of that name in Mardol as early as 1651 - whether on this site is not known. This building was known as the Harp by 1786 and was where the coaches to Welshpool started their journey.

By 1820 the inn was known as the Britannia - a name it was to keep until about 1985. By 1828 regular coaches ran from there to Aberystwyth and during the summer period to Barmouth. It was also the terminus for carrier's carts from Montgomery and Ryton-IX-Towns in the middle of the 19th century.

After the death of her husband James Edwards in March 1839 Mrs Edwards announced her intention of continuing to manage the inn, *"endeavouring by her own greatest personal exertions to uphold the high character which her late husband established for this house; and she hopes in her bereavement to receive the sanction and patronage of her friends."*

For many years it was the home of the Gullet Club. The club was founded in the Gullet in Hill's Lane on 24th February 1785, with meetings held every Tuesday evening between six and ten when each member paid two pence towards a quarterly dinner. The club flourished and soon had over fifty members, but after a disagreement with the landlord of the Gullet Inn the club moved to the Britannia, holding its first quarterly dinner there on 29th July 1845. Seventy-five members sat down to dinner on the 15th April 1847 and we are informed that they enjoyed, "A baron of beef, a noble joint which had not been cooked in the town for many years." The main guest on this occasion was the Mayor Mr. John Legh. Another special event took place in April 1848 when a whole sheep was roasted and the Mayor Mr. C. Lloyd was present. Around 1870 the rules of the club changed and it adopted political associations, which alienated many members and led to its closure in 1872.

In 1900 The Britannia was owned by the Right Hon. Earl of Tankerville but was looked after by his agents Messrs How & Son. The landlord was James Bray who used to brew and bottle his own beer and ale. The inn had twenty-six rooms. Five were for public use and thirteen were used to accommodate thirty guests overnight but there was only one urinal and toilet to serve the whole hotel. There was accommodation for twenty horses in the stable yard and you could enter the inn from the yard, from Mardol Quay or from Carnarvon Lane.

The hotel was purchased around 1988 by Henri Quinn and his wife Liz who over the next ten years sensitively up-graded the business, changing not only its image but also its name from the Britannia to the Shrewsbury Hotel. They retired from the hotel trade in 1998 selling the business on to JD Wetherspoon, a national pub chain, for a deal said to be worth more than £900,000.

Photo: The Britannia Mardol c.1946

THE ARMOURY c1995

An historic building with a modern spacious and light interior with fine views over the river Servern. Unique relaxed "library" and "reading room" interior.

Theme	Delightful and unusual airy open plan hostelry.
Opening Hours	Mon – Sat 12.00 – 11.00 Sun 12.00 – 10.30
Licensee	Andrew Barker & Denise Miller
Address	Victoria Quay, Victoria Avenue, Shrewsbury.
Contact	T. 01743 340525
Brewery	Brunning & Price
House Beers	Wadsworth 6X, Woods Shropshire Lad
Real Ales	Shropshire Lad & guest real ales
Food	Wide range of excellent food from sandwiches to four course meals. You'll need to book at peak times!
Wine	Wide choice of wines. Over 50 malt Whiskeys demanding serious attention
Promotions	None
Entertainment	Conversation – it's music free!
Accommodation	None
Awards	None
Customers	Unusually varied bunch of people of all ages.
Comments	A good safe place to meet and dine with your friends. Large open plan interior ideal for large groups.

HISTORY OF THE ARMOURY

When first erected this building stood between the Wenlock and London Roads on what is still known as Armoury Gardens. It was designed by a Mr. Wyatt and built in 1806 at a cost of £10,000. The two-storey building is 135 feet long and 39 feet wide and was erected to store the arms of the volunteer corps of Shropshire and the surrounding counties. Inside the building were two magazines for storing ammunition. Several small houses were built around the perimeter to house the storekeeper, armourer and subaltern's guard and their families. But ten years after it had been opened local author Thomas Howell reported, *"few arms of any description had been deposited there"*, and the jobs of the men required little or no work.

When first erected it was described as "a handsome brick edifice," but within fifty years of being built, the arms were removed to Chester, the building lay unoccupied, looked very dilapidated and had been purchased by Lord Berwick. In 1916 a group of people living in the area cleaned, painted and furnished the building, turning it into a hostel for families of Belgian refugees who had been displaced during the First World War.

In 1919, Morris's were relocating their head office and other departments from New Street to the Welsh Bridge site. They needed a bakery and as building material was scarce after the First World War they purchased the Armoury, dismantled it and accurately rebuilt it as their bakery on the banks of the River Severn.

Morris's baked bread there until about 1959 when production was moved to a new site in Abbey Foregate, leaving the Armoury to concentrate its effort making cakes and confectionery, mainly for the wholesale trade.

Early in 1995 a £400,000 restoration project was started to restore the building to its former glory and to open it up for new enterprises. The upper floor with its gallery of wooden beams was offered as office space, while the ground floor was taken over by a Cheshire based family run business called Pubs Ltd. who turned it into an up-market bar and restaurant.

Photo: Inside the Armoury when it was used by Belgian refugees in c.1916

75

SOHO c1861

This pub is now a cocktail bar, the interior was completely renovated in 2002 in a contemporary style. The new licensees are determined that this family run business will offer a high standard of home cooked food with fresh local and seasonal produce

Theme — A pub refurbished into a cocktail bar and restaurant.

Opening Hours — Mon Sat 11.00 - 11.00 Sun 12.00 - 10.30

Licensee — Rob & Lorraine Teasdale

Address — Smithfield Road, Shrewsbury

Contact — T. 01743 236887

www.historicalhostelries.co.uk

Brewery — Free house

House Beers — Carling, Extra Cold Stella, and Creamflow.

Real Ales — None

Food — Excellent meals in contemporary surroundings

Wine & Spirits — Wide choice of cocktails and wine.

Promotions — Selected Cocktails two for the price of one 5pm - 8pm and all night Monday.

Entertainment — Thursday Night is for Goths

Accommodation — None

Awards — None

Customers — This will tend to appeal to younger people on their way to the night clubs that are in the area. During the day the quality of the food should attract a substantial trade.

Comments — Customers of SOHO enjoy good cocktails prior to dining. They are not looking for a traditional pub.

HISTORY OF THE SOHO BAR

This inn was first recorded as the Globe, the name being transferred there in 1861. The original Globe Inn stood on Castle Hill but the name was transferred to the house on Smithfield Road after the old building was removed from the site of the railway station.

The name was changed to the Smithfield around 1916 to reflect the close proximity of the cattle market and again in 1964 to the Proud Salopian after the market was removed to Harlescott.

The Proud Salopian was named after Thomas Southam a local businessman who owned a large brewery in Chester Street on the site now occupied by the Gateway Education Centre.

He first started trading as a merchant of wines, spirits and ale from premises on Wyle Cop before acquiring the Chester Street brewery, which he built up to supply public houses throughout Shropshire and the surrounding counties. In 1851 he was elected for the first time to the Stone Ward and was to remain a councillor for the next forty-four years, taking great pride from the fact that during that period he was elected on four occasions by his peers to be Mayor of Shrewsbury. His first term of office was from 1865 to 1866, he was re elected to serve between 1871 and 1872 and finally for a double term between1884 and 1886. For the next forty years a sign hung outside the inn with a fine portrait of Mr. Southam, dressed in his mayoral robes.

In 1886 the landlord of the Globe was William Gittins and like so many publicans at that time he had another trade to supplement his income. He was advertised as a cutler working from 127 Frankwell where he also repaired umbrellas and re-seated cane chairs guaranteeing good workmanship and the best materials.

By 1900 the inn was owned by Trouncer's Brewery from Longden Coleham, who were Thomas Southam's greatest rivals in the town. There were five public and five private rooms with accommodation for six men in three rooms. The customers were described as mostly from the labouring class and women, perhaps suggesting more "ladies of the night." There was a house in the yard at the rear and stable accommodation for fifteen horses.

In 2004 the inn was completely refurbished and the name changed to the Soho.

Photo: The Globe c.1890

THE ALBERT c.1856

A traditional pub offering a good standard of traditional ales. It is currently being refurbished and is soon to have a new landlord.

Theme	Traditional town pub with a live music
Opening Hours	Mon - Sat 11 - 11 Sun 12 - 10.30
Licensee	Bill & Cheryl Haynes
Address	Smithfield Road, Shrewsbury, SY1 1PB
Contact	T. 01743 358198
	www.thealbert.tk
Brewery	Banks's
House Beers	Banks's Bitter & Mild & local guest beers
Real Ales	Yes
Food	Unknown
Wine & Spirits	General selection of wines & spirits
Promotions	Not known
Entertainment	Live music is a feature of the Albert
Accommodation	2 Single and 1 double room available
Awards	None
Customers	Cross section of locals and visitors
Comments	Very conveniently located near the Rail and Bus stations with excellent beers and local guest bitter available.

HISTORY OF THE ALBERT

Smithfield Road was constructed around 1835 but does not appear by name until listed in the directory of 1856. Until the creation of Priory Road it was the only thoroughfare within the loop of the river to be called a "Road," the rest being referred to as "Streets." The road was built for, and named after, the new cattle market.

The Albert was named in honour of the Prince Consort. It would have been built around this period and is first mentioned in the 1856 directory. It was erected on part of the old town defences a section of which can be seen in the wall in Meadow Place.

In 1900 the inn was a free house and was owned by William Williams, a builder, who lived just two doors away. The inn had seven private and three public rooms and overnight accommodation for two people in a double room. Its customers were described as mostly dealers and farmers.

In 1900 Richard Gough became landlord taking over from Samuel Morris and starting a family link with the inn that lasted three generations. Mr. Gough transferred to Smithfield Road from the Plough in Frankwell and was a tenant for four years until he purchased the Albert with all its fixtures and fittings from Mr. Williams for £4,100. An interesting inventory listing the entire fixtures and fittings of the inn was drawn up by Hall, Wateridge & Owen at the time Richard Gough became landlord. It came to £328-3s-8d and the items included seventeen gallons of brandy, three gallons of Irish whiskey, four and three quarter gallons of Scotch, three and a half gallons of gin, sixty-one gallons of cider, thirty-five gallons of old ale, and twenty-six and a half gallons of port.

The Gough's brewed and bottled their beer up until 1913 and had a brew house with sufficient barrels to hold up to 600 gallons of beer. Brewing would often start at two o'clock in the morning and although the ale that they brewed would be stored in a cellar that often flooded; this was a blessing in disguise as the moist earth kept the walls of the cellar cool. Richard was followed by his son Sidney until 1957 when grandson Ken Gough became landlord.

Photo: Carnival day outside The Albert Smithfield Road c.1955